GARDEN
harvest

GARDEN
harvest

Steven Bradley

with photography by
JO WHITWORTH

LAUREL
GLEN

SAN DIEGO, CALIFORNIA

contents

introduction

Spring is usually the busiest time of the year in the garden. After the long winter months, the plants behave as though they have to make up for their dormant period in record time. Leaves and shoots start to emerge overnight, and some plants impatiently flower before their leaves have even had time to open. This is followed by summer, the most colorful time of year. Plants ensure the survival of their species by producing seeds, and in order to do this, they must flower. This provides the gardener with the opportunity to create a constant display of color, as well as a healthy and varied source of food for the table.

In spite of all the hard work, both spring and summer are times when the garden can be enjoyed thoroughly. Pleasant weather means that the gardener can spend long periods of time in the garden, either working or relaxing. Time spent sitting enjoying the garden can be an opportunity to observe new plants and planting designs at close quarters, noting any failures or disappointments, and planning for the future. There are always new projects to be undertaken, new techniques to master, and new constructions to be built.

Garden Harvest contains a selection of ideas and projects for gardeners who want to make the most of the growing season, expand their existing garden designs, or bring about gradual changes and improvements to their gardens. This book is a perfect gardening companion throughout the growing season, from the first days of spring when you are planning for the busy coming months and caring for the early-flowering plants, to the heady days of summer when you are pruning, propagating, and cultivating your garden produce. *Garden Harvest* illustrates the best way to grow fruits, vegetables, and herbs in your own garden. It examines the advantages of both organic and conventional methods of culture, so you can choose which is best for you. There are also practical projects to demonstrate various new techniques,

illustrations to show how to plan the garden layout, and tables packed full of useful information about propagation as well as fruit and vegetable care.

Once you put the techniques and ideas from this book into practice, your garden will become not only a stunning visual spectacle but also a symbol of the fruit of your labors.

Steve Bradley

OPPOSITE *The coral pea plant,*
Hardenbergia leguminosae *produces
deep purple flowers and fruit.*

ABOVE *The vivid red fruit of the
red currant,* Rubus rubrum, *will add
a splash of color to any garden.*

RIGHT *An apple tree grown in a container
provides a perfect contrast to the green
foliage surrounding the pergola and
seating area.*

BELOW RIGHT *Squashes are fast-maturing
vegetables that can grow to be very
large, but it is best to harvest them before
they grow too big.*

BELOW LEFT *Sunflowers provide a riot of
color when they open. These tall-standing
flowers are effective when planted in an
annual or herbaceous border.*

shoots
OF SPRING

Spring is the time of greatest opportunity in the garden because events that take place during these few months will influence considerably how well the garden emerges, develops, and matures over the coming year. Action taken now will affect both the soil and the plants.

The trouble is that there is so much to do and so little time to do it—there are hardly enough hours in the day. After weeks of relative inactivity spent planning, preparing, and waiting for the weather to improve, it suddenly does, and things start to happen at a fast pace. The plants (including weeds) cannot wait to get started, and those well-laid plans turn into a total blur of frenetic activity as ideas are finally put into operation.

Timing is critical. The gardener needs to watch the weather in order to get an early start and to avoid the spring frosts. The risks of starting too early are high, however, since some plants may be killed by a cold spell, whole crops of fruit lost, while other plants may respond to low temperatures by starting to flower before they have had time to develop fully.

Once the plants start to grow, it is possible to take measures to ensure that natural growth can take place unhindered for as long as possible. A plant's development is measured by its need to reach a certain stage of growth in order to trigger the next stage of development. Any hindrance in growth will cause stress conditions and have a bearing on growth and yield. Understanding how each plant works and what its basic needs are will help the gardener.

You may think you can tell what the weather is about to do, but spring is definitely the most unpredictable of seasons. Wildly fluctuating temperatures rise pleasantly high at noon, only to plunge below freezing in the early hours of the morning. Coupled with the likelihood of strong winds and heavy rain, it all makes life difficult for the gardener, the plants, and those well-laid plans—but then, that's all part of the fun!

RIGHT *The hardy flowers of cherry on naked branches are often seen as one of the very first signs of the passing of winter and the coming of spring.*

early stages of growth

The majority of the plants already established within the garden will have had a rest during the winter months. This will have been either a true period of dormancy (where the plant will have shut down completely) or an enforced spell of partial dormancy. The latter case affects a great number of trees and shrubs, and occurs when the cold climate prevents their tops from growing, even though there may have been some root activity and growth actually taking place within the relative warmth of the soil.

ABOVE *Small-flowered narcissuses cope better with wet, windy, spring conditions than large ones, although the delicate flowers look unable to withstand harsh conditions at all.*

Winter shutdown

This winter shutdown is signaled within the plant by the shortening days of autumn. A large number of flowering and fruiting plants need a period of cold temperatures (not necessarily freezing) in order to stimulate chemical changes within them. These changes will influence the development of the flower buds and the quality of the flowers, which will then open in the following spring and summer.

Even after this chilling has taken place, many plants undergo an additional period of relative inactivity until other changes occur to trigger and promote the new season's growth. The flowers, which lie deep in the buds of shoots formed during the previous summer and autumn, continue to develop slowly until a few days before growth starts, with the reproductive parts of the flowers often being the last to form.

First signs of life

The start of a new season's growth is determined by an increase in the hours of daylight, rather than the warmer air temperature, of a spring day.

However, although the longer days signal the actual start of growth, it is the temperature of the surrounding air and that of the soil where the plant's roots are that will dictate the rate at which growth progresses once it starts. That is the reason plants may start to grow at exactly the same time each passing year (to within a few days). The speed at which they grow from then on will depend on whether the spring is "early" (with warm days and warm nights, encouraging rapid early season's growth) or "late" (where the cold, wet conditions provide the plants with a much slower and steadier rate of growth early in the season).

Another complication for the observer is that the growth of the plants below ground and above ground usually starts at slightly different times, balancing out within the very first few weeks of growth, rather than

occurring simultaneously. Nowhere is this more obvious than on plants that produce a full display of flowers before a single leaf has emerged.

Although most plants are "primed" for growing, there is still no cast-iron guarantee that the coming year will be a successful one. Even the hardiest of plants will produce new growth, which is vulnerable to damage from frosts, high winds, or the battering force of heavy rain until it has fully developed and hardened. Flowers, in particular, are prone to this type of damage, because they are so much more delicate than the surrounding stems and leaves.

A large number of plants will also face mounting pressure from below ground level as the soil gradually becomes warmer. Most have a minimum soil temperature requirement, and once the temperature climbs above this, root activity begins. Spring root growth in plants can start up to six weeks before there are any discernible signs of growth on the above-ground parts of the plant. Therefore, even though the plant still appears to be dormant, there may be a large amount of growth activity taking place, either below ground or inside the shoots and stems, where it is invisible to the naked eye.

ABOVE *Daphnes flower early, and often it is the heady perfume that makes the gardener (and the insects) seek out the flowers.*

BELOW *Although individual blooms may not last long, they do not all emerge at once, and this phased emergence gives the impression that the flowering period is longer.*

Physiological plant growth

Once plants have started to grow, the rate of their growth will be quite rapid, with some two-thirds of the annual growth occurring during spring and early summer.

LONG- AND SHORT-DAY PLANTS   Unlike gardeners, who think of time in terms of days and months (calendar time), plants work in physiological time. Their development is measured by their need to reach a certain stage of growth or development in order to trigger the consequent stage of their development. For example, fruit trees like apple will produce the embryos of the following year's fruit buds at around the end of July or the beginning of August in calendar time. However, in physiological terms, the important criteria is the time when the current year's shoot growths have developed approximately 22 leaves.

In most plants, the trigger for a whole range of growth phases (such as the start of stem growth, flower development, and the formation and swelling of bulbs and tubers) is greatly influenced by the number of daylight hours they are exposed to. For example, a large proportion of plants that flower in the first half of the growing season can be regarded as "short-day" plants. They are plants whose flower buds develop during days of 12 hours of daylight or less. Other plants, such as chrysanthemums and dahlias, naturally flower in the second half of the growing season, and can be regarded as "long-day" plants, since their flower buds need 12 hours or more of daylight in order to develop successfully.

ABOVE   *The embryo flower buds that have produced these young apples formed on the tree the previous summer.*

BELOW LEFT   *Witch hazel and snowdrops coming into flower are a sure sign that before long, other spring-flowering plants will start to emerge for the new growing season.*

BELOW   *Curly green kale is a cabbage variant. It is edible but is increasingly grown for its ornamental value.*

In reality, many of these "long-day" plants need short days for leaf and stem growth, and only after a number of leaves have formed are they able to respond to the longer days. This is one reason plants that are put in the ground late or seeds that are sown late will produce fewer flowers and less fruit. They cannot catch up with those planted at the correct time.

PROLONGING GROWTH Once plants have started to grow, it is important to ensure that natural growth can occur unhindered for as long as possible. Any break in growth caused by factors such as drought, waterlogging, windy conditions, erratic watering, cold periods, or root damage will cause stress conditions for a plant. This results in an interruption of the plant's growth pattern which will ultimately have a bearing on growth and yield. With perennial plants this can have a detrimental effect not only in the current season but also in the following year, particularly if the stress period occurs when the plant is forming next year's flower buds or tubers.

Fruiting plants, such as tomatoes, can be induced by the gardener to start flowering slightly earlier by keeping the plants slightly dry when the first truss is flowering. However, once the fruit has started to form it is crucial to keep the plants well watered at all times.

ABOVE *This hardy cyclamen is a very resilient plant, lying dormant in dry, shaded conditions for much of the year, and emerging to flower in late winter and early spring.*

BELOW *Some plants, like the crocus, appear to be very soft and delicate, but are in fact active during a relatively short growing season. Many changes are taking place in the parts of the plant hidden underground.*

working garden diary
The onset of spring is a busy time for the gardener. Listed here are many of the main jobs to help the gardener plan and implement a successful growing season, and enjoy a fruitful harvest.

GARDEN AREAS	LATE SPRING/EARLY SUMMER			MIDSUMMER
TREES, SHRUBS, AND CLIMBERS	Prune, feed, and mulch roses, trees, and shrubs. • Move and replant shrubs before full growth. • Cut back the old wood of neglected shrubs to	ground level. • Trim winter-flowering heathers and remove green shoots from variegated plants and upright shoots on weeping plants. •	Spray roses against black spot and apply a general fertilizer. Look out for aphid attacks. • Prune spring-flowering shrubs immediately after flowering.	Look out for aphid attacks and spray now, before the population increases. • Prune ornamental cherries
VEGETABLES	Sow seeds of main-crop peas, cabbages, lettuce, beets, and carrots. • Plant main-crop potatoes, cauliflowers, and cabbages. • Pinch growing tips of flowering broad beans. • Make further sowings of beets, cauliflower, spinach, radishes, carrots, main crop peas, broad beans, and a	second sowing of parsnips. • Sow curly, crisp lettuce, cilantro, basil, sea kale, dill, summer savory, green onions, and nasturtiums. • Sow tomatoes for growing outdoors within the next two weeks. Choose cherry types if growing in a hanging basket and bush types if growing in	patio containers. • Remove and compost plant residue from overwintered crops such as winter cabbages, kale, and brussels sprouts. • Sow eggplant, celeriac, peppers, and self-blanching celery under protection (a heated greenhouse) for an early start.	Make further sowings of main-crop peas, cauliflower, radishes, spinach, beets, carrots, broad beans, and a second sowing of parsnips. • Take semiripe cuttings of rosemary and thyme. • Sow quickly maturing green onions and spring cabbages. • Sow sea kale to overwinter for next year's summer crop. • In a nursery seedbed, sow
FRUIT	Complete mulching of fruit. • Apply a liquid feed to fruits grown in containers. • Apply nitrochalk to black currants. • Introduce bouquets of flower blossoms around the base of fruit trees to encourage fruit pollination and ultimately fruit set. Avoid applying any sprays until flowering is over as	sprays may be toxic to pollinating insects. • If fruit is growing on a sheltered wall, remove winter protection and prune fan-trained figs. • Finish pruning gooseberries, plums, and red currants. • Train canes of blackberries. • Use healthy prunings from gooseberries and red and white currants in	order to make hardwood cuttings and produce new plants if required. • Ventilate both cloches and tunnels over strawberries. • Continue to hand-pollinate and provide frost protection for fruit trees trained on walls.	Cut down the old fruiting canes of raspberries to ground level and tie in the strongest of the young canes. • If harvesting early apples, eat within a few days of picking as they will not keep. • Complete summer pruning of bush and cordon gooseberries, and red and white currants. • Continue to liquid-feed fruits growing in containers. • Ventilate cloches and tunnels over strawberries to protect them from the birds.
GREENHOUSE/ CONSERVATORY	Plant early indoor tomatoes. Be prepared to protect from late frosts. • Start hardening off bedding plants gradually, replacing the frame lights at night only if temperatures fall below 37° F. • Sow seeds of summer bedding plants. •	Take cuttings of geraniums or buy plug-plants as they come into garden centers. • Prepare the greenhouse border for tomatoes. • Cover the glass in a greenhouse with sacking if frost is forecast. • Provide shade for plants with large	leaves, e.g., *Cineraria*, as they often wilt in full sun. Liquid-feed them once a week. • Plant hanging baskets and patio planters with bedding plants. Be sure to water them well throughout the summer.	Pinch growing point when five or six trusses of tomatoes are developing per stem. • Harvest tomatoes and cucumbers regularly in order to encourage fruit production. • Continue to train and remove side shoots. • Take cuttings of
GENERAL TASKS	Plant dahlia tubers as well as early chrysanthemums. • Lift, divide, and replant herbaceous perennials. • Continue to feed the birds regularly to reduce the damage they do to plants while foraging for their food • Start your weed-control program as soon as weeds	emerge because they often harbor pests and diseases (groundsel = rusts, mildew, and aphids; chickweed = red spider mites and whiteflies). • Paint the growing tips of bindweed as soon as they emerge, as they are at their most vulnerable then. • Keep	frost protection covers handy in order to cover tender plants if a late frost is forecast. For low-growing plants, a light mulch or covering of soil should suffice. • Protect the tender shoots of young plants from slug and snail damage with a mulch of sharp gravel.	Support plants as growth extends • Pinch all but five strong shoots on large-flowered chrysanthemums. Debud extra-large flowers, leaving the crown bud • Lift, divide, and transplant flag irises after flowering • Weed and deadhead half-hardy annuals • Deadhead roses (not those grown for
PESTS AND DISEASES	Start a spraying program to control fruit pests and diseases. • Spray flowering almonds and peaches against	leaf-curl disease. • After pruning, spray roses against black spot. • Control slug and snails now—killing off the first	generation as they hatch from eggs will prevent the population from building up early in the year.	Spray asters and roses regularly against mildew. • Keep inspecting plants for pests and control as necessary. • Spray apples to

14 shoots of spring

soon after flowering. • Continue spraying roses to combat black spot. • Loosen ties on trees and climbers if	they are cutting into the bark, check tree stakes and replace them if required. • Remove suckers from roses.	Tie climbing roses; untie and prune rambler roses and weeping standards. • Screen newly planted conifers to	protect them from winds. • Move deciduous trees and shrubs at leaf-fall. • Plant or move evergreens during mild	and showery weather. • Remove mulch from around roses and replace with fresh mulch in spring after pruning.
a good keeping onion for transplanting next March. • In colder areas, during early July, plant leeks sown in a cold frame in January. • Continue to pinch growing tips of flowering broad beans. • The beginning of midsummer is the lastest you should sow beets, carrots, lettuce, turnips, spinach, and parsley. • To prevent wind	rock, draw soil up around the stems of winter greens (particularly kale and broccoli). • Plant sweet corn (must be planted in a block). • Sow turnips for spring greens, Japanese onions for harvesting next June, and spring cabbage in nursery rows. • Harvest main-crop onions, ensuring the bulbs are ripened before storing.	Plant spring cabbages into their permanent positions. • Sow spinach for cutting in April. • Tie onions in ropes as soon as the bulbs are ripe. • Lift potatoes for storing, and beets and carrots sown before July. • Finish earthing up celery before severe frosts. • Pull up tomato plants with fruits still attached and store in a frost-free place to ripen. •	Green fruits may be wrapped in paper and stored in the dark. • Tidy up the vegetable plot, removing all debris. • Lay out grapefruit skins to attract slugs and snails, as killing the adults now will reduce the numbers of both overwintering adults and eggs, and hence protect seedlings and new plants. • Lift main-crop potatoes,	carrots, and beets, and store in a cool, dark place. Leave later sowings in the ground and lightly thin recently sown crops. • Cover string beans with plastic cloches to protect them from frost and extend the cropping season. • Plant garlic. • Sow early summer cauliflower and turnips under winter protection. • Sow broad beans for next year's crops.
• Support the branches of apple, pear, and plum trees bearing heavy crops. • After both fan-trained peaches and nectarines have fruited, cut laterals back to replacement shoots and tie these in. • Thin both apples and pears after natural fruit drop if the fruit set is heavy. • Sever runners from strawberry plants and plant. • Prune restricted forms of apples and pears near the end of midsummer. • Gather early pears while still slightly underripe. •	Remove dead and weak branches from pitted fruit trees if necessary. • Continue layering strawberry runners and planting well-rooted ones into their permanent positions for the following year's maiden crop. • Clean up existing strawberry beds after cropping, including cutting off the old leaves at 4 in. above the crown. • Prune plum, greengage, and damson pyramids.	If fruits come off the fruiting spurs easily, pick midseason apples and pears, but use damaged fruits immediately. • Lime the soil if necessary. • Summer prune restricted forms of apples and pears in wetter areas. • Plant bought strawberry runners by the end of the month. • Continue to pick apples and pears, and	check fruits in storage, removing any showing signs of rotting. • During late October, cut down old-fruited blackberry and hybrid berry canes and tie in the young canes. • Prune cherries (fan-trained, bush, or tree) by cutting out some old wood. • Order fruit trees, canes, and bushes. • Remove ties from	fruit trees grown as spindle bushes once the cropping branches have set in a horizontal position. • Apply grease bands to the stems of fruit trees and spray them with a winter wash as the leaves start to show their autumn colors.
tender perennials used for summer bedding, such as gazanias and penstemons. • Cool greenhouse and transfer pot plants grown for spring flowering to a shaded frame. • Pot up cinerarias, calceolarias, and primula seedlings sown in July for spring flowering. •	Take nonflowering shoots of pinks, heathers, and rock roses as semiripe cuttings; insert in either pots or trays, and place in a cold frame. • Take cuttings of fuchsias and pelargoniums.	At the end of the month, lift and pot perennial bedding plants such as heliotrope and fuchsias. • Continue to liquid-feed pot plants, switching to a fertilizer high in potash. • Take cuttings of hardy shrubs and tender perennials. Root them in the greenhouse and pot up rooted heather cuttings.	• Pot annuals sown under glass in midsummer. • Clear growing bags and replant with winter lettuce plants or strawberries. • Harvest green tomatoes and store them in the dark to ripen. • Cover grapes with muslin to protect from wasps. • Bring plants inside that were moved	outdoors for the summer, including late-flowering chrysanthemums. • Remove shading. • Sow sweet pea seeds to overwinter in the greenhouse. • Clean, repair, and insulate the greenhouse, ensuring heating works well.
their hips), removing a third of the flowering stem. • Deadhead dahlias. • Apply fertilizer to all deadheaded plants. • After they flower, cut delphiniums down to 4–6 in. • Shorten wisteria growths to 6 in. from the base. • Trim hedges such as Berberis thunbergii, hawthorn, beech, escallonia, privet, and thuja at the end of the growing season.	• When this season's growth ends, trim formally clipped hedges, pittosporum, laurel, elaeagnus, hornbeam, holly, chamaecyparis, and box. • Lift spring-flowering bulbs about six weeks after they have flowered, dry, then store. • Continue to deadhead and water herbaceous perennials.	Order seed catalogs. • Tidy up herbaceous borders. Dead stems may be left for added protection but they should be shortened to reduce wind rock. • Plant evergreens toward the end of the month if conditions are cool and moist. • Deadhead and weed herbaceous borders. • Lift	dahlias when blackened by frost. Cut down the stems, label the tubers, and place them upside down to dry. • Order deciduous trees and shrubs (including roses and hedges) now for late autumn delivery. • Large, dense clumps of peonies may be divided, but they may not	flower for a year or two after lifting. • Prepare planting sites by double digging. • Take hardwood cuttings from roses and set them two-thirds deep in a v-shaped trench in a sheltered border. • Lift and plant rooted cuttings in their permanent positions this time next year.
prevent codling moth attack. • Spray roses against rose rust and, in wet seasons, spray outdoor tomatoes against blight. • Remove and burn	tips of gooseberry and black-currant bushes that are infected by American gooseberry mildew.	Continue spraying roses to control black spot and	mildew. • Spray peaches and flowering almonds against	leaf-curl disease just before the leaves start falling.

planning
A GARDEN

Gardens tend to be projects that are gradually developed over a long period of time. Within the overall plan, some of the plants selected will be short-term, possibly lasting less than one full season, as with some types of bedding and edible salad crops. Others—such as roses, trees, shrubs, some types of fruit, and even vegetables like artichokes or asparagus—may occupy a place in the garden for many years.

To some extent, a garden can be left to develop as it wishes. It will still look quite attractive and produce a kind of harvest, and a few gardeners are satisfied with that approach. However, in order to get the maximum benefit and productivity from a garden, it is best to try to work within some kind of system or method.

This approach involves some degree of planning to ensure that all of the space within the garden is fully utilized, to reduce the risk of the spread of pests and diseases, and to prevent the soil from becoming overworked. There can be other objectives behind the planning, such as laying out the garden for ease of maintenance and accessibility and, where possible, to make as many of the tasks as possible within the garden a pleasure rather than a chore.

Perhaps the most limiting factor for most gardeners will be their soil—the type, lime content, percentage of clay or sand, and the rate of drainage. All of these can be modified, but it does take time and planning to do this. Improving soil is a long-term project but is worth it since it will have a major impact on how the garden can be managed, the range of plants that can be grown, and how well those plants will establish and perform. It is preferable to improve the soil over an area, rather than just in a localized point at the base of each plant. But *any improvement* will benefit the plants' growth.

RIGHT *Having soil with a pH range between 7 and 8 enables you to grow a wide range of plants within the garden.*

soil

When deciding whether to grow plants organically or by using manufactured fertilizers, it is worth bearing in mind that both systems produce good plant growth, but there can be significantly different effects on the soil. Organic systems provide lower levels of nutrition, but greatly improve soil fertility and biological activity. While nonorganic systems improve nutrition, they may not be as beneficial to the soil over the long term.

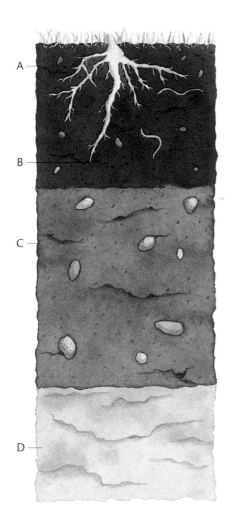

Soil structure

Although often taken for granted, soil is the gardener's raw material and the success of a garden may hang on it. The quality of the soil is reflected by the quality of the plants growing in it—poor soil can only produce poor plants. Over the course of thousands of years, soil forms into several layers: a cross-section down through the soil, called a "soil profile," shows that the darkest, most fertile topsoil is to be found in the surface layers; the paler, less-fertile subsoil forms the middle layer; and the palest parent material, or rock layer, lies below that (see *Anatomy of soil layers*, left).

Soil management

One of the most essential components of successful gardening is careful soil management: taking care of the soil to maintain and improve its fertility in order to provide a balanced, healthy environment in which plant roots can function, grow, and develop.

Managing soil is far from easy. It involves a number of separate but closely interlinked factors, such as how to prevent structural damage to the soil and maintain a balance between the spaces around the soil particles where both air and water are found. Keeping a soil healthy and improving soil fertility involves more than just providing plants with the right nutrients in the appropriate amounts. They also include creating a healthy environment for a thriving, organically rich community of beneficial organisms, such as bacteria, fungi, insects, and worms. These organisms will feed on the organic matter and plant debris in the soil, breaking them down into forms that are available as food for the resident plants. Even the bodies of these beneficial organisms, when they die, become part of the plants' food.

The food, or nutrients, used by plants can be divided into two main categories, depending on how much a plant needs. The major nutrients are the essential building blocks of plant structure and activity. Although the minor nutrients may not appear to be as vital, all the nutrients are needed for overall balanced, healthy plant growth (see the *Plant Nutrients* chart, pg. 19).

If any one nutrient is in short supply, causing a deficiency within the plant, the plant will not fulfill its true growth potential even if other nutrients are in plentiful supply. (See chapter 4, *Benefits of Organics,* on how to add missing nutrients and, specifically, project 6 on the ways to test your soil.)

All soils are slightly different, even though they are composed of the same basic constituents—they will behave differently depending on which plants are growing in them, and how and when (if at all) they have been cultivated. Some plants are hungrier than others and take more nutrients out of the soil while others, such as peas and beans, harness nitrogen from the atmosphere and store it in their roots. This stored nitrogen can be used by these plants or by future crops as the old roots gradually decay. Vegetables, in general, take lots of nutrients out of the soil, mainly because when harvested, much of their bulk is removed, so very few nutrients are returned to the soil, breaking the cycle of decay and reuse.

ABOVE *Dwarf string beans and other members of the legume family not only produce an edible crop but also harness atmospheric nitrogen and store it in their roots. This will eventually be released into the soil for other plants to use.*

PLANT NUTRIENTS	
Major nutrients	**Minor nutrients**
Nitrogen	Manganese
Phosphorus	Copper
Potassium	Zinc
Calcium	Boron
Magnesium	Molybdenum
Sulfur	Iron

BELOW *Growing vegetables in formal beds of a fairly uniform size has the advantage of making crop rotations and planning much easier to organize.*

ABOVE *Cultivations, such as fine raking, are ideal for working the soil down to a fine texture, in order to create a seedbed or planting area for propagating vegetables and hardy annual bedding plants.*

BELOW RIGHT *Heavy clay soils, especially those containing very little organic matter, will eventually dry out and form deep cracks in dry weather. This causes a severe loss of soil water from a much greater depth.*

BELOW *Double digging is hard work but is a good investment of time, especially if some well-rotted manure is incorporated, as this will encourage greater worm activity within the soil.*

Soil cultivation

Any operation involving the movement or disturbance of soil can be regarded as a form of cultivation. Gardeners have been cultivating their soil for about 10,000 years, but for many modern gardeners, one of the most contentious issues is how and when to cultivate their precious garden soil and, for a growing number, whether to cultivate at all.

There is little doubt that cultivating causes some structural damage to soil. This may only be very slight on an annual basis, but it can have a cumulative effect over a number of years. To make matters worse, if soil is cultivated when it is either too dry or very wet, the damage caused can be quite serious and have a detrimental effect on the plants that are grown in it. Cultivating the soil too frequently can also cause damage to the structure and merely walking over wet soil can create compaction, which may lead to poor soil drainage.

DEEP CULTIVATION Any soil cultivation deeper than 8–10 in. is regarded as a form of deep cultivation. Deep digging is a practice that can be beneficial in heavy and compacted soils, because it enhances drainage and improves conditions in the root zone. It is often used as a starting point for cultivation by gardeners even if they decide not to cultivate their soil on a regular basis.

Double digging is a method of deep cultivation that is more effective for improving drainage than improving fertility—incorporating the subsoil with the topsoil is much more likely to dilute the fertility of the topsoil rather than stimulate the fertility of the subsoil beneath. With double digging, deep

ABOVE *Many vegetable crops only need weed control until they are established and their leaves cover the soil, blocking out light (which stops weed seeds from germinating).*

cultivations are carried out every three or four years to break up the subsoil and allow deep penetration of plant roots. Manure may be added during these cultivations. In this way, deep cultivation is beneficial because it encourages plants to send their roots deeper into the soil, which in turn helps the plants cope better with dry weather.

Deep beds are dug in preparation for long-term cultivation. The area is dug deeply with plenty of organic matter added as part of the process. In future years, very little cultivation is practiced, but fresh layers of organic matter are added to the surface each year, to be incorporated by worms.

SHALLOW CULTIVATION Shallow digging with either a fork or a spade, raking, hoeing, and even tamping with your feet to firm the soil, are all forms of shallow cultivation. This cultivation practice is often carried out to break down the soil clumps into smaller clumps and particles in order to make seed sowing and planting easier. It also buries crop debris and weeds to leave a "clean" surface for the next plant population.

BELOW *For ornamental plants, decorative mulches such as stone or gravel not only help to control weeds, retain moisture, and deter slugs and snails, but can also be used to form an attractive covering.*

Shallow cultivation carried out through a crop, or between growing ornamental plants, is often aimed at keeping the soil surface free of weeds and reducing competition between the plants the gardener wishes to grow and their indigenous rivals, which endeavor to share the available water, nutrients, and space. In many respects, soil cultivation is a way of managing soil so plants are more easily started, grown, and harvested; but in a healthy soil with a balanced growing system, cultivation is not essential.

Drainage

Plants need water—without it, they are unable to function. Water is the key element that triggers the chemical changes to occur inside each plant. The availability of air and water to a plant's roots is controlled, to a large extent, by the drainage of the soil. It is the gardener's responsibility to make sure that the soil is appropriately drained, and in order to do this, there are several drainage techniques from which to choose.

THE IMPORTANCE OF DRAINAGE   When a soil has plenty of water, much of it is held in the spaces between the soil particles or as a very thin film of moisture over the individual soil particles. It is from these specific places that the plant draws water to function and grow. How freely a soil drains will depend on the size of its particles. Clay has very small particles, each one surrounded by a film of moisture; this is the reason that clay soils have the capacity to hold large quantities of water. On the other hand, sandy soils have fewer, larger particles, which means that they hold far less water and are free-draining, having a tendency to dry out completely in periods of hot weather.

For the roots of most plants to function well, they need both air and water present in the soil. If a soil becomes so wet that it is "waterlogged," air is then excluded from the soil and the roots are unable to function for long before they die—they quite literally suffocate. In fact, if the soil is too dry or too wet, the plants will suffer, not just from a lack of air or a lack of water, but also a lack of nutrients. Remember, plants do not "eat" nutrients from the soil, they "drink" them in a solution. Other factors connected with a lack of air do not affect the plant immediately. Without air, the organic matter in soil is unable to break down and release its mineral plant foods, and the bacteria involved in this process need air in order to stay alive and active. Waterlogging not only stresses plants, it also makes them quite vulnerable to certain types of pests and disease. For instance, fungal diseases—such as clubroot in cabbage or redcore in strawberries—thrive in poorly drained soils.

Perhaps one of the most peculiar consequences of draining a soil is that it actually improves the capacity of the plants growing in it to resist dry conditions, because they tend to form deeper root systems in well-drained soil. In places where the water level is high, plant roots tend to be shallow, since they are restricted to areas that are not waterlogged. In inevitable periods of drought, these shallow-rooted plants are restricted to drawing their water from a layer of warm, dry surface soil. Unfortunately for these particular plants, surface soil dries out all too quickly.

ABOVE Soil that is constantly waterlogged for more than a few days will seriously affect plant growth. Oxygen will not be able to reach the roots, which will restrict the uptake of both nutrients and water.

BELOW Wet soil can provide the ideal environment for numerous soil-borne fungal diseases such as redcore, which kills healthy strawberries and can live in the soil for up to 12 years.

DRAINAGE SYSTEMS The term "water table" refers to the zone in the soil that is usually wet for at least six months of the year, and if this zone is too close to the surface, some form of drainage system will be necessary to lower the water level. Drainage systems are usually arranged in a herringbone pattern, with trenches 2–2½ ft. deep. The floor of the trench slopes gradually toward the lowest point in the garden, and branch drains join the main drain. Before the trench is refilled with soil, place a layer of gravel over the pipes to intercept the water in the soil and direct it toward the pipes. If there is an outlet, such as a ditch or stream, the drain can flow into this. If not, it may become necessary to construct a dry well, which is a pit that is typically filled with gravel, into which waste water is piped so that it drains slowly out into the surrounding soil.

Other methods of improving soil drainage include double digging (see project 2). Raised beds can also be used in order to lift the plants above the waterlogged areas of soil. In cases where the garden slopes steeply, a system of flat beds or terraces can be built, but before this can be achieved, a series of levels must be measured in order to establish the steepness of the slope, and you must calculate how much soil would need to be moved.

All the above drainage techniques are very arduous tasks, but will greatly benefit the soil in the end.

ABOVE *Long-term drainage problems can be permanently solved by installing drains to take away the excess water and lower the water table in the soil.*

BELOW *Raised beds are an effective way of growing better crops if the garden is low-lying or has nowhere to which to drain the excess water.*

leveling a slope

It is important to check vertical and horizontal surfaces to ensure that they are "true," that a consistent, desired fall or slope is maintained over a site. A carpenter's level will provide an accurate reading in smaller areas and survey equipment can be rented for larger areas. However, using this type of equipment can be daunting the first time around and it may not always be necessary. There are times when it is possible to improvise with basic gardening equipment.

A simple but effective level can be achieved by plugging a short length of transparent plastic tubing vertically into the end of a garden hose and laying the hose on the sloping site. By filling the hose with sufficient water until it shows in the vertical clear plastic tube, you can establish and record levels across the site. Since water level remains constant, the level in the clear plastic tube will always match the level at the highest point of the hose and can therefore be used for marking identical heights. The advantage of this method is that levels can not only be determined over long distances but also can be established and recorded around obstacles and bends.

If you do not have a piece of transparent plastic tubing on hand, simply fill the hose with water, and at the bottom end of the slope, hold up the end of the hose and gradually lower it. When water first starts to seep out of the end of the hose, then the hose end is at the same level as the top of the slope.

AUTHOR'S TIP:
Dividing a slope

If the slope is much longer than the length of the hose, divide the slope into equal parts, moving the hose to record the levels of each section.

CLOCKWISE FROM TOP LEFT

Start by rolling out a hose along the slope to be measured, and at the highest point, insert a 3-ft. cane or stake vertically into the soil.

Using a piece of twine or string, tie one end of the hose to the cane or peg at the top end of the slope, ensuring the end of the hose is approximately 3 in. above ground level.

Run the hose down the slope and, at the lowest point to be measured, insert a second 3-ft. cane or stake vertically into the soil.

Using several pieces of either twine or string, tie the lower end of the hose to the cane or stake, with the end of the hose and plastic pipe tied up to the vertical cane or stake.

From the top of the slope, slowly pour water into the hose, making sure to allow time for air bubbles to emerge. Keep filling the hose until the water overflows from the uppermost end of the hose.

Walk down the slope and look at the point where the water level has settled. If this is not easy to see, a small amount of vegetable dye can be added to the water. The water level can then be recorded on the vertical stake; this point should be level with the top of the slope.

TOOLS FOR THE JOB

1 hammer

1 watering can

MATERIALS

1 garden hose

Two 3-ft. canes or stakes

Several pieces of twine or string

1 transparent plastic pipe

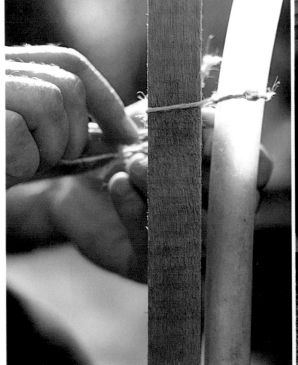

double digging

With double digging, the soil is cultivated to a depth of two spade blades. This technique is most frequently used on land that is being cultivated for the first time or where a hard subsurface layer (called a "pan") of soil has formed, impeding drainage and the penetration of plant roots.

This method of digging improves the friability of the subsoil without bringing it nearer to the surface, so the most biologically active layer of topsoil is always closest to the young roots of cultivated plants. It is very important to avoid mixing the subsoil with the topsoil. If the two are mixed together, the fertility of the topsoil is diluted, rather than improving the fertility of the subsoil.

Although this type of digging is hard work and can be very laborious, the benefits of double digging a plot can last for up to 15 years, provided the soil is managed correctly. To double dig an area so that deep-rooted plants, such as roses, shrubs, trees, or fruit trees and bushes, can be grown, a number of gardeners favor adding a layer of well-rotted manure or compost into the bottom of the trench before the topsoil is replaced.

In the vegetable garden, this organic matter may be laid over the surface of the soil after double digging; the compost will then be drawn into the topsoil by worms and insects. This way, the soil-borne bacteria and fungi break it down.

On heavier soils a layer of ashwood, sand, or gravel may be mixed into the bottom of the trench before the topsoil is replaced, to help improve drainage.

AUTHOR'S TIP:
Using a pickax

If the subsoil at the bottom of the first trench is very compact, it may be easier to use a pickax rather than trying to break through this layer with a fork.

CLOCKWISE FROM TOP LEFT

Starting at one end of the plot, mark off an area 2 ft. wide using a guideline and canes. Dig a trench to the full width and at a depth of one spade. If it is very large, the plot may be divided in two for convenience.

Remove the soil from this first trench and take it to the far end of the plot, laying it quite close to the area where the final trench is to be dug.

When all the soil is removed from the first trench, fork over the base of the trench to the full depth of the fork's tines.

If needed, compost or manure may be forked into the lower layer of soil or scattered on top of it after cultivation.

When the base of the trench is cultivated and the compacted layer broken through, mark off the next area 2 ft. wide with a guideline. Using a spade, start to dig the soil from this second area, throwing it into the first trench, while making sure that the soil is turned over as it is moved. This process will create the second trench and ensure that the base is forked over.

The process is repeated until the entire plot has been dug to a depth of about $1\frac{1}{2}$ ft.

TOOLS FOR THE JOB

2 guidelines

1 spade

1 wheelbarrow

1 fork

MATERIALS

8–10 3-ft. canes

Compost or manure

herbs for the garden

In times gone by, herbalists were important people within a community. They were the only people with the knowledge to help relieve everything from a stomach upset to the pains endured during childbirth. However, not all plants are beneficial and some people found herbalists to be quite threatening and powerful. As a result, many herbalists were persecuted as witches simply for knowing how to use the plants that grew near them. Recently, there has been a resurgence in the use of native and exotic herbs for both culinary and medicinal purposes.

LEFT *Although herbs are most commonly grown for their culinary and medicinal qualities, they also make very attractive ornamental plants, especially if they are allowed to flower.*

BELOW *Where space is restricted, some herbs can be grown upward by training them on canes or other types of support.*

Many things in life turn full circle, and the use of herbs as medicine is one of them. The advent of synthetic medicines saw plants largely ignored, but now that these medicines are ceasing to be the cure-all they were expected to be, more and more interest is being taken in the use of natural medicines as an alternative. It is an attractive prospect to be able to go into the garden and collect the ingredients of a cure for an ailment as well as those for the evening meal. No herb, however, should be ingested in any quantity without first getting the advice of a qualified herbalist.

Herb gardens of various shapes and sizes are becoming very popular as an attractive means of growing and enjoying the numerous herbs available. Most herbs are tastier and more effective when fresh, but they may not be in season throughout the year, particularly plants like basil, which hails from warm regions, or hardy species like rosemary and bay, which are tougher and less tasty in winter. Even a small herb collection will provide sufficient material to use both fresh and dry for use during the cold months.

ABOVE *Lavender makes an excellent path-edging plant, and in the summer, brushing against the foliage as you walk by will release aromatic oils into the air.*

Herbs tend to be spread widely across the plant classification groups, and range from trees such as bay, which will last many years, to tender plants like sweet basil, which are grown as annuals with a life span of just a few months. This diversity means that the herb garden needs to be planned very carefully in order to cover a long season of availability and allow each plant enough room to grow and thrive.

The other plants in the garden will also benefit directly from the presence of herbs growing among them or nearby. A large number of herbs seem to attract a wide range of beneficial insects, such as bees, which are drawn into the garden by flowering herbs like thyme and which will help to pollinate fruit trees in the spring. Fennel attracts hover flies, which are voracious predators of aphids and other small insects, and others, like pennyroyal, will deter ant activity; ants seem to dislike the scent of mint intensely and will avoid any plants near it too.

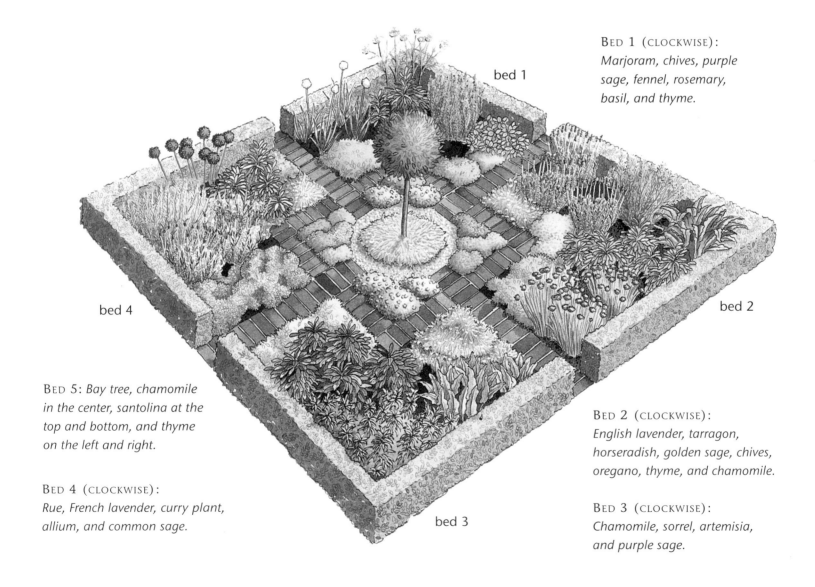

bed 1

bed 4

bed 2

bed 3

BED 1 (CLOCKWISE):
Marjoram, chives, purple sage, fennel, rosemary, basil, and thyme.

BED 5: *Bay tree, chamomile in the center, santolina at the top and bottom, and thyme on the left and right.*

BED 4 (CLOCKWISE):
Rue, French lavender, curry plant, allium, and common sage.

BED 2 (CLOCKWISE):
English lavender, tarragon, horseradish, golden sage, chives, oregano, thyme, and chamomile.

BED 3 (CLOCKWISE):
Chamomile, sorrel, artemisia, and purple sage.

herbs for the garden ❀ 29

vegetables for the garden

Nothing beats the flavor of freshly harvested, homegrown vegetables. They are currently more popular than they have been for a long time, even though the average garden appears to be getting smaller. The range of vegetables now available is wider than ever and more flexible in terms of size and harvest time. As more people become conscious of the various benefits of a healthy diet, greater quantities of vegetables are being eaten. People have also discovered the aesthetic attributes of a vegetable garden, because with careful planning, rows of beautiful, matching colors can be achieved.

BELOW *Vegetables do not have to be grown in rows, they can also be grown in a formal ornamental setting. Many have flowers and foliage that are attractive in their own right.*

One of the main reasons behind this resurgence in popularity is that more people want to know how plants are grown, and whether chemicals have been used during production, on the soil, or on the plant itself. The fact is, the only way to be certain the food you eat has been grown as organically as possible is to grow it yourself.

When planning a vegetable garden, it is very important to remember that plants must be divided into related groupings and that these groups should not occupy the same site in consecutive years—they must be rotated around the plot. This rotation cuts down on the need to fertilize the ground so heavily (different crops use nutrients at different rates) and also reduces disease transmission.

Growing your own vegetables gives you far greater control over what is eaten and, in particular, the quality of flavor. For instance, rather than selecting plants that give the maximum yield per square foot (which is what influences commercial growers), cultivars can be selected for a better or more distinctive flavor.

In addition to flavor, the growth pattern and harvesting period are also important considerations, especially where the aim is to reduce the need for storage to a minimum. Old cultivars will have lower yields than their newer counterparts but often the crop will reach maturity sooner and can be harvested over a longer period. Many of the new vegetable cultivars are hybrids, which may have a very brief harvesting period.

Another very important consideration when selecting plants to be grown organically is their resistance to pests and diseases. If chemicals are to be used as little as possible, any natural plant resistance has to be helpful to the gardener. This is where some of the new cultivars have the edge over old ones, and a good example of this is the carrot cultivar 'Flyaway' that has a natural resistance to carrot rust flies.

Of course, growing plants of any kind without using synthetic chemicals can also have its drawbacks and problems. If the conditions are favorable, a pest or disease can reach epidemic proportions quite quickly, and thus be difficult to eliminate purely by organic control methods. Also, some of the organic chemicals, such as derris and the pyrethrin-based products (that are favored by some gardeners), are just as harmful to a range of beneficial organisms, including ladybugs, worms, and fish.

Crop losses will generally be higher when organic methods of culture are used. This proportion of crop loss will vary from year to year, and may not be significantly higher than crop damage where chemical sprays are used. Growing vegetables organically is not necessarily more difficult than any other growing method, it is a matter of preference for each gardener.

ABOVE *Growing vegetables in beds has become more popular over recent years, and using such beds certainly makes planning and crop rotation more simple to manage.*

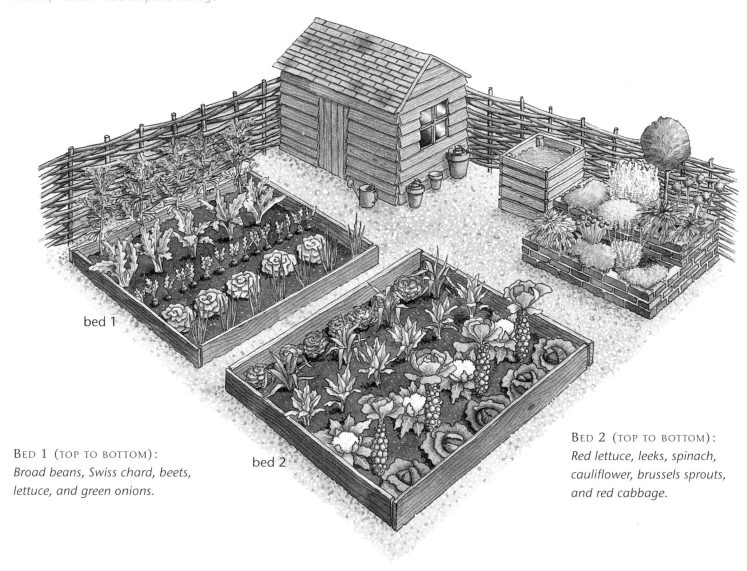

bed 1

bed 2

BED 1 (TOP TO BOTTOM):
Broad beans, Swiss chard, beets, lettuce, and green onions.

BED 2 (TOP TO BOTTOM):
Red lettuce, leeks, spinach, cauliflower, brussels sprouts, and red cabbage.

flowers for the garden

What is a weed and what is a flower? This is a subjective question. What one gardener chooses to throw out, another will care for and nurture. A large number of the plants that are grown in the average garden are "wild," but as native habitats become ever more restricted, at least these plants are being preserved. They also have the advantage of growing quite happily alongside the exotic ornamental plants introduced from other countries. As long as the harmony of the garden is respected, growing a mix of flowers will produce a spectacular result.

ABOVE *Borders of mixed plants that are encouraged to grow into one another give ornamental plants a semiwild appearance, even though the effect is quite contrived.*

How to classify native plants has kept botanists busy for years. Many plants that have naturalized over large areas are assumed to be native, but may actually have been present for only a relatively short period of time. For instance, the horse chestnut (*Aesculus hippocastanum*) and the sycamore (*Acer pseudoplatanus*) are so common in the United Kingdom they are now adopted natives, but they were in fact imported relatively recently.

As most modern gardening practices have become labor intensive and chemically dependent, it can be argued that returning to a regime based on cultivating native plants would be more environmentally friendly. Rather than using chemicals to guarantee the perfect, weed- and moss-free suburban lawn, creating a more natural look with longer grasses and wild flowers can be very attractive.

One considerable advantage of naturalizing plants in grass is the low maintenance factor. These plants, once established, virtually maintain themselves, and the grass need be mowed only once or twice each year. However, establishing these plants may well be the most difficult part of the process, since competition from the grass can reduce the growth potential of the new plants by as much as 30 percent until they are established. As with most seemingly natural gardening, a lot of care is necessary while preparing the garden, planting, and allowing a gradual evolution to a more natural state of affairs. This ground is just as likely as any other to be invaded by thistles, docks, morning glories, and other pernicious natives which, if neglected, can very soon destroy the whole scheme.

Once a garden consisting of predominantly native plants has established itself, the benefits are there for all to see and enjoy. A gradual encroachment of wildlife into the naturalized area (no matter how small) is one of the most enjoyable benefits; birds, insects, and small mammals will quickly make themselves at home. In time, their feeding habits can also contribute greatly to the management of the whole area.

A meadow may look very attractive, but do remember that unless it is managed with extreme care, one species can dominate the site, excluding the others through competition. The high proportion of flowering grasses in a meadow can also make life extremely uncomfortable for allergy sufferers during certain months.

A more moderate approach to creating a flower garden, at least to start with, is to naturalize both hybrids and cultivars derived from groups of plants, such as bulbs or herbaceous perennials, rather than depending solely on native plants. The range can be increased by introducing other plants gradually, as time passes and the gardener's confidence with the growing system increases.

ABOVE *Naturalizing bulbs in a lawn or other grass areas is a good example of "wild" or natural gardening.*

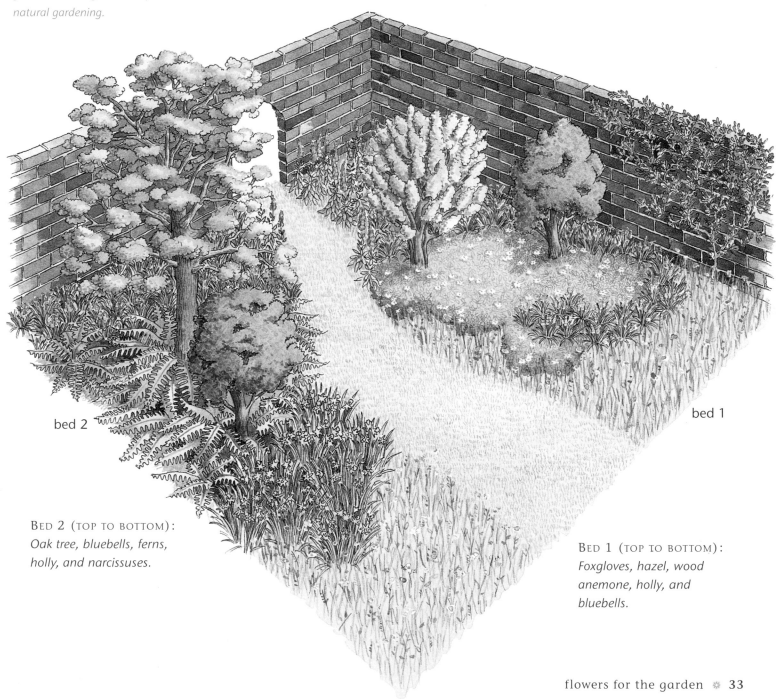

BED 2 (TOP TO BOTTOM):
Oak tree, bluebells, ferns, holly, and narcissuses.

bed 2

bed 1

BED 1 (TOP TO BOTTOM):
Foxgloves, hazel, wood anemone, holly, and bluebells.

flowers for the garden ❀ 33

saving space

The lack of land available for building means that modern gardens are being reduced to a minimum to accommodate more houses. This means that the enthusiastic gardener has to make the maximum use of the space available and be much more inventive with design.

It has become increasingly important to think in terms of three-dimensional, or "vertical" gardening, rather than being confined to the horizontal. If there is not enough room for plants to spread outward, then they will need to grow upward. By pruning regularly to keep their spread under control, there is no reason for a small garden to be any less interesting than a large one. Look for areas that can be planted upward as there will be numerous spaces even in the smallest of gardens. For example, the small space between a footpath and the wall of a building can be planted with dome-forming alpines and upright, narrow conifers, and there may also be room for a tightly clinging climber to establish itself against the wall. Even the cracks and joints between the slabs and pavers on a patio or driveway can easily accommodate tiny plants—if these small areas are not planted, the weeds will be quite happy to colonize them.

BELOW *In the wild, trailing plants can cover large areas of the ground, but in a garden situation they can be given the space they need by training them vertically.*

Window boxes, hanging baskets, and containers can be used in areas where there is no soil to make use of what is potentially "dead space" and, within the garden itself, canes, stakes, and obelisks can introduce height with roses and climbing plants growing up them. Make full use of walls and fences, but choose plants that can be pruned back, so that they do not grow forward and take up too much space.

Grow plants close together so that a sturdy one can act as a frame for a neighboring slow- or moderate-growing climber. Use plants with a long season of interest, two seasons of interest (spring flowers and autumn color for instance), as well as plants with different seasons that still grow together happily. Autumn- and winter-flowering bulbs under deciduous shrubs are a fine example of the latter, since bulbs in this group are only actively growing and flowering when the bushes have lost their leaves, and will be dormant when the shrubs are in leaf, so the shade does not harm them at all.

When growing edible plants, choose a mixture of slow- and fast-maturing crops, so that the room between young, widely spaced, long-term plants, such as brussels sprouts, can be occupied with a quick salad crop of radishes or green onions.

Storage is a constant problem in the garden, particularly when space is limited, so make the best use of what is there. The space beneath a raised deck can be used to store pots, containers, and tools, although the storage area will need to be waterproofed. Even furniture can do double duty, with bench seats used as storage boxes for tools or bags of compost.

ABOVE LEFT *Companion planting provides a slightly chaotic appearance, due to the wide range of plants being grown together.*

ABOVE RIGHT *Mixing edible and flowering plants together can give the garden an added dimension, and certain combinations make excellent companion plants.*

BELOW *Use scented stocks, dwarf lavender, and chamomile for a traditional combination of pastel colors.*

creating a raised bed system *Using raised beds*

for growing vegetables and herbs is an ideal way of incorporating a vegetable patch or "edible garden" where space is limited. With a larger garden the system remains the same, but the number of beds will probably increase. There are various benefits associated with growing plants in this way...

A raised bed will encourage plants to root deeper into the soil, which means that less watering is required. The plants can also be grown closer together and often in "square" planting arrangements rather than in rows. This will aid the production of slightly smaller vegetables that are ideal for people living alone or couples, rather than large families. However, bear in mind that root vegetables will often produce long roots due to the deeper root run of a raised bed.

Planting at such a high density cuts out the total amount of light that reaches the soil and thus reduces the development of weeds. This particular type of bed system will allow the growing season to be extended if necessary; it is easy to cover part or all of the bed with either clear plastic sheeting or garden fabric suspended on hoops that are fastened to the retaining wall of the bed.

The beds can be any length or height required, but the width of each bed is very important. The ideal width of each bed is 5–6 ft., so it is possible to reach the center of the bed from both sides, rather than having to walk on the soil in the bed.

AUTHOR'S TIP:
Adding soil to the bed

When adding soil to the bed, always mix it with the original soil since this helps water to be drawn up from the surrounding soil outside the bed.

CLOCKWISE FROM TOP LEFT

Mark the area and dimensions of the raised bed, and remove any surface vegetation. Level the soil along the lines where the timbers are to be positioned. Lay out the first layer of timbers to create a low wooden "wall" for the planting bed, and use a builder's square to check the right angles of the structure. Also, use a level to check that the timbers are level.

Repeat the process, working around the wall, stacking timbers to raise the height of the wall. Drive 6-in. nails into the corner joints on each layer of timbers in order to keep them stable.

When the wall has reached the required height, fix the top row by driving 6-in. nails at an angle through the vertical joints.

Turn over the soil inside the bed area. Add some extra soil and organic matter and mix it with the existing soil to aid drainage and water movement.

Tamp down the soil well enough to reduce uneven settling later when the plants are in place.

Finally, plant the vegetables and herbs into the new bed. These are usually planted slightly closer together than plants in rows in the garden.

TOOLS FOR THE JOB

1 builder's square

1 carpenter's level

1 hammer

1 fork

MATERIALS

Landscape timbers

6-in. nails

Organic matter

making a tomato growing-bag support

In recent years, there has been a dramatic rise in interest in growing food crops of all kinds in containers. These range from long-term plants, such as apple trees, with a life span of 15 to 20 years, to plants as fast-growing as radishes, which grow from seed to maturity in a matter of weeks.

Growing bags (a commercially prepared plastic bag of compost in which you simply have to cut holes) make convenient containers for short-term plants, such as low-growing vegetables, that will usually be in residence for only one growing season. Although often seen as short-term containers, there can be a fair amount of fertilizer residue left

in the growing bags at the end of the season, especially when plants such as cucumbers, peppers, and tomatoes have been grown in them. The bags can be used a second time to grow salad crops such as lettuce and radishes without the need for any extra fertilizer.

Unfortunately, it is common to encounter problems when growing tall plants, such as eggplant, cucumbers, and peppers, because the growing bag does not have the depth to allow for stakes to be used as supports. This can be overcome by making a frame around the bag and fastening the support structure to the frame, so that the plants grow up toward the support.

AUTHOR'S TIP:
Keeping the bag steady

The wire mesh floor of a frame will provide stability to the entire structure, since the weight of the growing bag holds the frame in place, which, in turn, holds the plant supports steady.

CLOCKWISE FROM TOP LEFT

To make the base, measure and cut two pieces of lumber to the same length and two pieces to the same width as the growing bag. Drill and screw the long and short pieces together in order to form a rectangle. Cut a section of wire mesh to cover the top of the wooden rectangle and staple the wire mesh to the edges.

Turn the rectangle over and drill one $5/8$-in. hole (about 3 in. deep) at each corner. Place the growing bag inside the frame and insert a sturdy cane into each of the drilled holes.

Draw the two canes at each end together, cross them to form a small V at the top, and tie them.

Tie a cane horizontally from one V to the other (just above the point where the canes are joined.) Next, tie long strings to the horizontal cane and lower them to the growing bag.

Place the tomato plants in the growing bag and water them well. Tie the strings around the base of each plant, so that as the plants grow they can be twisted around the string and it will provide support.

After three weeks of growth, the tomatoes will start to flower.

TOOLS FOR THE JOB
Measuring tape

1 saw

1 electric drill

1 pair of pliers

MATERIALS
4 pieces of lumber

1 growing bag

Screws

Wire mesh

Staples

5 sturdy canes or stakes

String

Tomato plants

tools &
EQUIPMENT

There are records of cultivation tools dating back to 40,000 B.C. and as horticulture has evolved, so too have the tools used to cultivate the plants that gardeners wish to cultivate and cherish. It is important to use good quality, well-made tools wherever possible, so that they will last for a long time. A good spade will last a lifetime, whereas a cheap one will last for a maximum of five years.

It is important to keep tools in good condition, by making sure they are kept sharp, and by cleaning and oiling them after use to prevent them from rusting. Never be tempted to try to use the tools for a purpose that they were not designed for; this will only strain and damage them, and make them less effective.

Before purchasing any tools, first decide what type of garden you want to create: a vegetable garden, lawn and flower beds, or a wildflower garden, for instance. Then list the most common tasks carried out in your chosen type of garden, starting with the most frequently performed tasks. Once this has been evaluated, make a list of the tools necessary to perform these tasks. This list will enable you to prioritize the tools that will be needed immediately and those you can acquire gradually.

Tools can be quite expensive. Therefore, when selecting tools, start by choosing ones that are frequently in use around the garden since those will be the most cost-effective ones. Tools that are used only for a very specialized purpose, or are used only once or twice each year, can be rented, as and when they are needed. In fact, if you are actually considering purchasing expensive power tools, it is advisable to rent the same make of tool (or a similar version) and try working with it before buying it. Renting tools is also a means of conserving valuable storage space.

RIGHT *A range of tools and a trusty wheelbarrow gathered for a working session in an area of the garden.*

essential gardening tools

Managing a garden is a multitask activity and therefore requires a wide variety of equipment. Depending on the season, certain tools are of more use than others. Most garden tools and implements fit into one of four categories: cutting tools, cultivation tools, general-purpose tools and equipment, and watering equipment.

ABOVE *A range of sharp, well-maintained cutting and pruning tools are an important part of any gardener's tool kit. The type and make of these tools will depend on their intended use.*

Cutting tools

POLE PRUNERS These are used for pruning branches that are almost out of reach, and can cut through branches up to 1¼ in. thick. They consist of a pole 6½–10 ft. in length, with a hooked anvil and curved blade at the tip. The blade is operated by a lever at the opposite end.

LONG-HANDLED LOPPERS Also known as "pruners," these are strong scissors-like tools with long handles, which give extra leverage when cutting thick stems or branches.

PRUNERS These are the best tools for most types of pruning. There are two basic types, depending on their cutting action. The anvil type has a single, straight-edged cutting blade closing down onto an anvil, which is a bar of softer metal or plastic. The bypass type has two curved blades passing each other very closely, cutting in a scissors-like fashion. A useful variation on some of the models that have an anvil cutting action is the ratchet type, which will cut through a branch in stages. They help reduce fatigue and are ideal for gardeners with small hands, though the cutting action is slower than that of conventional models.

SAWS Some pruning saws look similar to carpenter's saws but have two cutting edges: a coarse-toothed one for cutting live (wet) wood and a fine-toothed one for cutting dead (dry) wood. Many modern pruning saws can be folded and are intended only for cutting through smaller branches.

SHEARS Hand shears are available in several designs. Most have straight blades with a deep notch at the base for cutting thicker stems. Grass shears have a cutting action identical to hedge shears, but are designed for cutting lawn edges while they are upright. They have 2–3-ft. long handles, set at an angle to the blades.

Cultivation tools

FORKS AND SPADES These come in different sizes: digging (large), medium, and border (small). Most are fitted with a T, D, or YD handle grip, but those with long-handled shafts and no grips are increasing in popularity.

HOES There are two basic designs of hoe: the push (Dutch) hoe, which has a flat, D-shaped blade and is used almost exclusively for weeding, and the swan neck (draw) hoe, with a square or rectangular blade, which is used for weeding, turning, and furrowing when sowing seeds.

RAKES Most rakes have a single 6-ft. handle, though the head of a rake can vary in size and also in the number of teeth, from 10 to 32.

TROWELS AND HAND FORKS Most trowels are similar in design, with a miniature spade blade on a short handle. Hand forks may have three to five tines on a short handle.

ABOVE *Shallow cultivations, such as hoeing, often require light, long-handled tools with small, sharp blades that work just below the soil surface and only penetrate the surface of the ground slightly.*

RIGHT *Rakes are useful tools to lay out ornamental mulches of gravel around plants. The more teeth on the rake, the finer the soil surface can be raked.*

BELOW *For deeper cultivations, heavier and sturdier tools are required, with tines or blades that will penetrate down to a depth of 12–14 in.*

General-purpose tools and equipment

DIBBLE This tool is about 1 ft. in length and is often made from an old spade or fork handle that is sharpened at the tip. It is frequently used for planting seedlings. Similar tools with a steel cap over the point are also sold in garden centers and hardware stores.

GARDEN TWINE These are essential to the vegetable gardener. It is best if the twine can be wound on a special steel reel, which will keep it neat. Lines are used for marking out shapes of lawns and beds or as a guideline for seed sowing or transplanting.

MEASURING ROD This is usually homemade from a piece of straight, square lumber 6–8 ft. long, with marks at set intervals to aid rapid, reasonably accurate, measuring in the garden when planning and positioning plants.

SPRAYER Usually trigger-action and hand-held with a capacity of at least 1 qt. Sprayers are used to apply foliar food and liquid fertilizers, or to mist a greenhouse. Make sure that they are washed out thoroughly after use to avoid contamination.

WHEELBARROW The workhorse of the garden, the wheelbarrow is available with large, inflated, ball-shaped wheels, which is especially useful if the ground is soft. Compost, manure, soil, and all manner of tools and equipment can be moved around the garden more easily with the help of a wheelbarrow.

ABOVE *For deeper cultivations, it is important to use strong, well-made tools and equipment that can cope with the rigors of lifting and moving soil and other heavy materials.*

BELOW LEFT TO RIGHT *Trowels and hand forks are ideal for transplanting young plants, and the base of the handle makes a good dibble to firm soil around plant roots (left). Measuring and marking off are important, and a strong, brightly colored garden line held on a well-made spool will have many uses in the garden (center). A wheelbarrow is the workhorse of the garden and is the most commonly used method for transporting materials around the garden (right).*

Watering equipment

ELECTRONIC WATER TIMER Usually battery powered, these devices are ideal for programming automatic watering.

HOSE-END ATTACHMENTS These are interchangeable fittings with snap-on couplings for changing from one type of watering device to another. They are usually brightly colored in order to make them easier to see in the garden.

HOSES The basis of numerous watering systems, a garden hose with woven nylon mesh that is coated in plastic is much preferred when working at high water pressures.

SPRINKLERS
- Oscillating sprinklers: These have a central spray bar with a series of holes in the top and sides. On the side of the bar is a drive mechanism, which is driven by water pressure and moves the bar from side to side. The speed of oscillation is dependent on the water pressure.
- Rotary sprinklers: These have a number of nozzles on a central pivot, which rotate in a circular motion. Water coverage is usually very even and the rotary speed is governed by the water pressure.
- Rotary-hammer sprinklers: These sprinklers are based on a nozzle and counterbalance mechanism, which works to move the water jet in a series of short, swinging motions.
- Static sprinklers: These particular sprinklers usually consist of a spike that presses into the ground and a nozzle that delivers the water in a set pattern over one given area.
- Sprinkler and soaker hoses: These are basically perforated hoses. Some are flat with perforations on one side, which send out a fine spray over a 2½-ft. wide strip. Others just allow water to seep out at a very low pressure directly into the soil. They are very good for covering large areas and are often left in position permanently.

RAIN BARREL A means of water storage, this is especially useful for collecting rainwater to water acid-loving plants in hard-water areas.

WATERING CAN A good-quality watering can is essential for any type of gardening. A well-balanced can is one that starts to pour as soon as it is tilted, with a long spout for extra reach.

ABOVE *Many hose attachments, such as spray nozzles with a trigger action, are ideal for watering pots and trays of plants.*

BELOW *There are many different methods of applying water to the garden. Some are more efficient than others.*

APPLICATION RATES FROM SOME WATERING APPLIANCES

Appliance	gals/hour
Hose, 45 ft.	145–265
Lawn sprinkler	80–170
Soaker hose, 90 ft.	15–30

benefits
OF ORGANICS

Although soil is an organically and structurally complex material, it often gets taken for granted. It is seen by many as just something that plants live and grow in, but a healthy soil is the most important asset that any gardener can have to work with.

It is possible to grow some plants without using soil at all or to grow plants in soil but use only inorganic fertilizers or pesticides to keep them growing. However, many gardeners are convinced that plants grown by these cultural methods rarely do well or, in the case of edible plants, tend to lack the flavor of produce grown under balanced growing conditions.

There is nothing new about gardening in an organic way. The whole concept is based on the principle of working with nature rather than against it, by using natural methods to maintain soil fertility rather than relying on chemicals to do the job. For most plants to fulfill their growth potential, they need to have an organic relationship with the soil or compost in which they are growing. This involves the natural recycling of plant and animal waste to feed the plants (at least in part) and the encouragement of soil-borne organisms to incorporate these waste materials into the soil. This not only helps the plants to grow but maintains the soil's natural chemistry and improves the physical and structural characteristics, as well as the overall performance, of the soil.

One reason for rotating the crops in a vegetable plot is because different plants extract different nutrients at varying rates from the soil. Various gardeners seek to avoid or strictly limit the amount of inorganic material they use, simply because they prefer to grow plants "naturally." Others opt to grow purely organically because they are concerned about the possible accumulation of inorganic material, such as pesticide residues, and its potentially harmful effects.

RIGHT *The benefits of organic gardening are particularly apparent when growing vegetables like garlic, because there are no chemical residues left over from pesticides or fertilizers.*

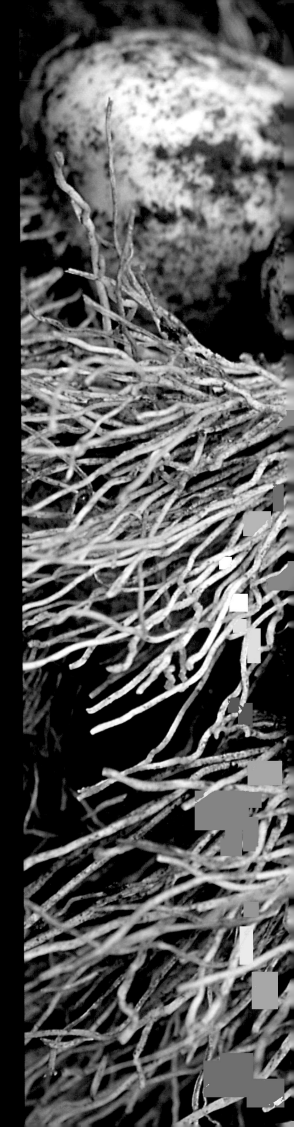

the science of organics

A large number of gardeners are now growing their own food, or at least a portion of it, mainly in an attempt to obtain produce that is free from pesticides. Concerns over chemical residues in the soil are leading more and more gardeners to turn to organic cultural methods of growing as an alternative to chemicals.

A soil that is both balanced and fertile should be populated by millions of microorganisms. As part of their life cycle, these microorganisms will feed on organic matter until they die, decay, and finally release nutrients back into the soil. The plants will then draw on that extraordinary reservoir of nutrients in order to produce both a balanced and healthy growth.

Organic methods of growing both plants and food closely follow those basic biological principles that are found in nature. Instead of merely feeding plants with fertilizers, the gardener must pay particular attention to feeding the soil the plants are growing in. A well-fed soil, in turn, can feed the plants, thus achieving the gardener's endeavor to grow and produce chemical-free food in a safer environment.

ABOVE *Using composters to collect and process organic waste is an excellent way to recycle plant residue and improve the fertility of the garden soil.*

THE ELEMENTS OF A COMPOST HEAP

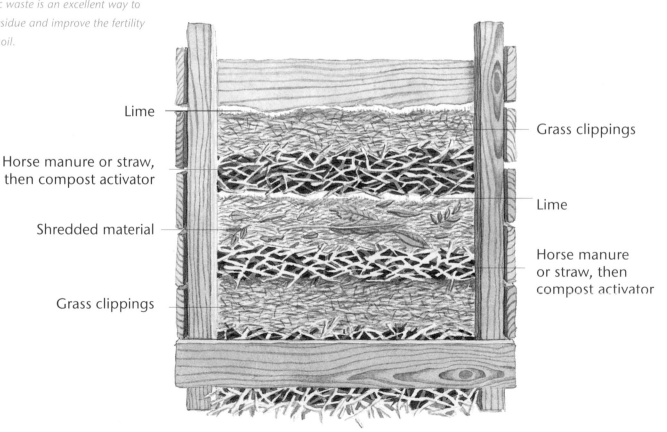

Lime

Horse manure or straw, then compost activator

Shredded material

Grass clippings

Grass clippings

Lime

Horse manure or straw, then compost activator

The nitrogen cycle

Generally speaking, a healthy soil is one that has plenty of soil organism activity, and keeping the soil well supplied with large quantities of dead plant residue will stimulate this. The vast majority of the plants grown by gardeners are capable of obtaining major elements, such as nitrogen, from the actual soil or compost in which they are growing. A supply of nitrogen, to be found in several forms, is maintained in the soil as a direct result of the nitrogen cycle.

When plants and animals die, they decompose and are incorporated back into the soil. They are then broken down by insects and worms, and subsequently by the bacteria and fungi that are living in the soil. This process releases nitrogen as well as other elements, which in turn become available in various forms that plants are able to use. A number of plants, including members of the pea family (*Papilionaceae/Leguminosae*), are capable of trapping nitrogen from the atmosphere and using it to help them grow, storing it in nodules on their roots.

ABOVE *Legumes, which are members of the pea family, harness atmospheric nitrogen, storing it in small nodules, or root swellings. It is released into the soil as the plant decays.*

pH scale

Nitrogen and other plant nutrients will be available to the plant in different quantities depending on the soil conditions. Soils can be either acid, alkaline, or neutral, and this has a bearing on what plants can be grown in them. Acidity and alkalinity are measured using the pH scale, which ranges from 0 to 14. A pH of 7.0 is neutral (neither acid nor alkaline).

BELOW *Testing the soil to determine how acidic or alkaline it is can be the starting point for deciding how to improve and manage the soil and what plants to grow in it.*

pH SCALE

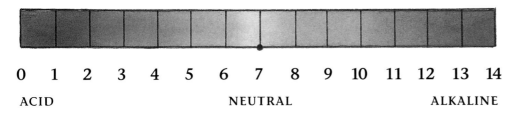

0 1 2 3 4 5 6 7 8 9 10 11 12 13 14

ACID   NEUTRAL   ALKALINE

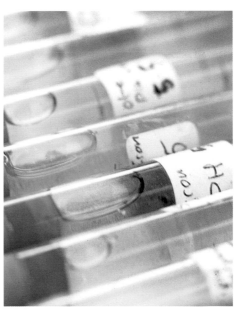

The scale is logarithmic, so that a pH of 3.0, for example, is 10 times more acidic than a pH of 4.0. For most plants, a soil pH of around 6.5 is generally preferred. Very few plants will actually grow in soils with either a pH value that is above 9.0 or a pH value that is below 4.0. Most natural soils range from pH 4.0 to pH 6.0.

The main reason most gardeners aim to keep their soil pH between 6.5 and 7.0 is because a maximum amount of nutrients is readily available to plants within that specific range and so they will be able to grow the widest range of plants.

ABOVE *Vegetables like these onions benefit from the addition of organic matter because it improves the soil structure and rooting environment.*

Organic gardening techniques

Growing plants organically is not a new concept. For generations, farmers and gardeners have recycled waste by spreading muck over a field, digging in manure, or applying well-rotted organic material as a mulch to be drawn into the soil by worms and insects. They have also returned crop residue to the soil—vegetable trimmings, leaves, and roots will all return nutrition to the soil. This is part of the very basis of crop rotation. By rotating crops of unrelated species, it is possible to recycle nutrients while minimizing the risk of any pests or diseases surviving.

SOIL ENRICHMENT   One of the main advantages of adding organic matter to the soil is that when it decomposes, organic acids are produced. These in turn help to release nutrients, which are already present in the soil, but may not be available to the plants. For this particular reason, materials, such as farmyard manure, are often credited with having a much higher fertilizer value than they actually contain.

Another benefit to incorporating material, such as well-balanced and well-rotted farmyard manure, into the soil on an annual basis is because it gives the top 6 in. of soil absorbent qualities. It can increase the water available to plants by up to 25 percent in the first year and by 60 percent in the second year. Scientists have also found that incorporating organic matter that is a mixture of chicken and cow manure plus waste paper into soil contaminated with pesticide residues will attract sufficient populations of beneficial bacteria and fungi to break down up to 90 percent of the residues within one year.

There is little doubt that adding organic matter to the soil will help to improve its overall structure and therefore the plant's rooting environment. However, a major dilemma for any gardener is the knowledge that such cultivations have a tendency to destroy the soil's natural structure. For this specific reason, some gardeners will reduce the cultivations to a bare minimum, perhaps only disturbing the soil to plant a new crop or to prevent weeds from establishing, and they will mostly rely on any organic matter being incorporated into the soil naturally.

Many gardeners wishing to add organic matter to the soil will do so in the autumn. The material may be left on the surface or incorporated into the soil, but the rate at which it is broken down will be greatly influenced by the activity of soil organisms. Their own activity, in turn, will be influenced at this time of year by the temperature of the soil in the top 6–8 in. Earthworms are at their highest level of activity when the soil temperature is around 50° F, and they will travel to deeper levels in the soil

and rest (hibernate) when soil temperatures become either too high or too low. Most bacterial activity in the soil will cease altogether when soil temperatures fall below 42° F. Because the soil will drop to its lowest temperature in the month of January, very little breakdown of organic material will take place at that particular time, but it will be restimulated as the soil warms up in the spring. By applying thick layers of organic matter in the autumn when the soil is warm, the insulating effects of this material will keep the soil warmer for a longer period of time and will also help to extend the active period of the soil organisms.

ORGANIC CONTROLS The soil definitely benefits from fewer chemicals being added to it. For example, some pesticides that are applied to the soil are known to act as a skin irritant to earthworms, which will discourage them considerably. This, in turn, will affect soil structure, the amount of air entering the soil, and the incorporation and breakdown of any organic matter in the soil. It is therefore crucial to take all the necessary steps to make the soil as "worm-friendly" as possible, using organic means of control.

ABOVE *Organic mulch made up of wood chips is a natural method of protecting these cabbage seedlings from both frost and weeds.*

BELOW *Plants extract nutrients from the soil in various quantities, so regular crop rotations and growing green manures on fallow areas will keep the soil in good condition.*

Even if chemicals are not applied directly to the soil, they can still have an effect on it. Every time a plant is sprayed with a pesticide, it is inevitable that a proportion of the chemical will drip from the plant onto the soil. Therefore, using organic pesticides will benefit the root zone of the plant as well as the area being sprayed.

Although organic pesticides are derived from natural products, this does not mean they are entirely harmless and some may actually harm beneficial insects. As the search for alternative control measures goes on, there is a strong possibility that, in the future, gardeners will continue to spray their plants, but the majority of the "chemicals" they use will be based on natural biological extracts.

• Organic sprays: These sprays can be based on fatty acid extracts from plants or rapeseed oils, and they operate in different ways. They can immobilize the pest until it dies of starvation or block its breathing pores, ultimately causing suffocation. In addition, some sprays work on the basic toxicity principle of an organic poison, which disrupts the pest's metabolism and kills it. For many of the fungal problems that attack plants, organic sprays based on lime or copper mixtures are preferred by most organic gardeners. Effective controls for certain fungi, based on sprays containing milk, are also now being tested as an easy alternative all over the world.

• Barriers and traps: These can be very simple, such as a saucer of milk or beer, which will attract slugs and snails and cause them to drown. Others offer the pest a place to hide, such as an overturned pot of straw on a stake that earwigs will use. Once captured, the insects concerned can either be released away from the garden or exterminated. On a much larger scale, vulnerable crops can be grown in isolation by surrounding them with a wide band of a plant that repels the pest. One long-established trap works by using a scent (or "pheromone") that draws flying insects to it, where they are then trapped on a sticky surface.

• Biological control: This involves the use of one naturally occurring organism to control another that is causing a specific problem for the gardener. For instance, eelworms of different species can be introduced to parasitize slugs or vine weevil grubs in order to cause complications, such as bacterial infections, which will kill the pest. This particular method has been used to control certain insects for years. There is even a bacterial spray that is sprayed onto brassicas to kill caterpillars when they feed on the crop.

• Resistant cultivars: For many years, plant breeders have striven to produce cultivars of plants that have a built-in tolerance or resistance to some of the major pests that attack them regularly. This resistance can work in different ways; some cultivars of plants have been bred with longer hairs on the leaf surface, which makes it quite difficult for insect pests to crawl over them and mount an attack. Other plants have been specially selected because they contain low levels of the chemicals that attract insects to them to feed or lay their eggs.

• Companion planting: Various plants are natural insect repellents, while others have allelopathic properties, which means that they are capable of producing chemicals that repel other plant species. These specific plants will often provide some protection to crop plants if they are grown close by. Some crops, called "sacrificial crops," are maintained for that sole purpose and they can be the same plants that are used to draw pests away from the main crop. Trap plants with sticky stems and leaves are also very useful companion plants.

trench composting
A compost trench is a simple alternative to a compost heap. It can reduce the number of times the organic matter needs to be handled, and is an easy way to accumulate and use plant debris in order to keep a plot within the garden looking neat and tidy.

Almost any plant or kitchen waste can be added to a trench at any time of year, making this a method preferred by most gardeners for use over the autumn and winter months, when temperatures are low and a compost heap may not be very active. The compost trench is an efficient way of disposing of old plant material, provided it is relatively free of residual pests and diseases, particularly soil-borne diseases such as clubroot of brassicas, onion white rot, parsnip canker, or potato cyst eelworms. Often, several trenches can be open and in use at the same time to cater to the crop rotation system within the vegetable garden and to reduce the risk of pests or diseases carrying over from one crop onto the next.

Probably the most convenient place for trench composting is in vegetable plots, because vegetable gardening takes a lot of nutrition out of the soil, and this loss must be replaced to feed the next crop. Another favorite place for trench composting is the site of new rose, tree, and shrub borders, in order to improve soil fertility.

AUTHOR'S TIP:
Dealing with slugs

Trench composting encourages slugs, since they tend to feed on the decomposing matter and lay their eggs close by. This can be overcome by watering the compost with an antislug solution, which will kill eggs and adults, or by using grapefruit peel as bait to kill slugs that feed on it.

54 ❋ benefits of organics

CLOCKWISE FROM TOP LEFT

In late summer or early autumn, mark off the area that is to be dug over in a series of trenches, and mark the lines of the first two parallel trenches.

Dig a single trench about 1 ft. wide and deep, and move the soil from the trench to the end of the plot, which will be the very last section to be trenched.

As they become available, gradually fill the trench with plant debris, vegetable scraps, and kitchen waste.

Dig a second trench in a similar way to the first one. Cover each additional layer of material in the first trench with the soil that has just been dug from the second parallel trench.

After the first trench is full and the second trench has been dug, start filling the second trench by creating a third trench. Each completed trench will gradually settle over a month or two as the plant material decomposes.

Woody material, such as prunings or cabbage stems, will decay faster if it is shredded before being buried, and a small amount of nitrogenous fertilizer may also need to be incorporated to speed up the whole process.

TOOLS FOR THE JOB

Marking pegs

Garden twine

1 spade

1 fork

1 shredder

MATERIALS

Plant debris

Vegetable scraps

Kitchen waste

Nitrogenous fertilizer

ABOVE *Sweet corn is a heavy feeder and likes to grow in a fertile, well-drained soil. Planting it in blocks helps to produce a better crop, since it is wind-pollinated.*

Organic materials

The basic difference between manures and fertilizers is one of bulk. Indeed, relatively large amounts of manure are used, providing only a small quantity of nutrients, though they do give the added bonus of some minor nutrients and fiber, which is converted into valuable humus. Fertilizers are used in relatively small quantities because the plant nutrients they contain are in a concentrated form.

BULKY ORGANIC MANURES Incorporating bulky organic matter into the soil will supply it with both nutrients and fiber. The green vegetation, as well as manures with animal waste, will provide small quantities of nutrients almost immediately, but little fiber (see chart below showing the average percentage of a given nutrient in a sample of the materials listed). Woody and fibrous material is a much better choice for opening heavy soils and improving soil structure, while on lighter, free-draining soils, providing these materials will improve moisture retention. These materials are ideal if the aim is long-term soil improvement. Indeed, as they decompose they will ultimately contribute to the formation of humus, which in turn absorbs other applied nutrients.

In order for bulky organic manure to provide the greatest amount of nutrients, it should be applied when only partially rotted; if not, most of the nutrition will have been washed away before the manure is even applied. It is important to understand that the longer manures are stored, the lower their nutritional value.

PERCENTAGE OF NUTRIENTS (APPROXIMATE)			
Material	**Nitrogen (N)**	**Phosphate (P)**	**Potash (K)**
Garden compost	1.5	2.0	0.7
Leaf mold	0.4	0.2	0.3
Chicken manure	2.0	2.0	1.0
Cow manure	0.6	0.3	0.7
Horse manure	0.7	0.5	0.6
Pig manure	0.6	0.6	0.4
Sheep manure	0.6	0.3	0.7
Turkey manure	2.0	1.5	1.0
Mushroom compost	0.6	0.5	0.9
Seaweed	0.6	0.3	1.0
Sewage sludge	1.0	0.6	0.2
Spent hops	1.1	0.3	0.1
Wood ashes	N/A	0.6	6.0

Organic matter can be added to the soil by growing a crop and digging it into the topsoil, which is known as "green manuring." These fast-maturing crops are dug into the ground about six to eight weeks after germinating, as a means of improving both organic matter and nutrient levels. The release of nitrogen is quite swift and so provides an early boost to plant growth; but the greener and younger the manure, the less fiber is produced and so the less the soil will be affected.

The bulk of a plant's organic matter is a carbon-based product of photosynthesis. Only about 5 percent of the plant's bulk is made up of nutrients that were taken from the soil. In effect, a green manure returns much more to the ground than it has taken out and will eventually form humus within the soil.

To make this type of manuring work effectively, it's important that it is planned as a "crop" to fit in with other crop rotations. For example, a crop of early potatoes can be followed by a green manure of mustard, which is then incorporated into the soil before planting a crop of winter cabbages. In effect, the nitrogen in the soil is being recycled by the mustard, rather than being washed away by leaching. The mustard also suppresses weeds, and some gardeners are convinced that the presence of mustard will help to attract some root-eating plant pests, which will be killed when the green manure is incorporated.

With crops of rye grass, there is little nutritional value to be gained from sowing in the fall—the most noticeable improvement comes from spring sowing. This crop should be mowed regularly and dug in the following winter, with the plant's fibrous root system greatly improving the structure of the soil. It should be remembered that in the long term, green manuring is not an effective substitute for regular applications of organic matter.

ABOVE *Comfrey is a perennial plant, often grown as an annual green manure in order to prevent the soil's losing nutrients.*

NITROGEN IN GREEN MANURES	
Green manure	**Nitrogen**
Borage	1.8 %
Comfrey	1.7 %
Mustard	1.7 %
Red clover	3.0 %
Rye grass	1.2 %

BELOW, LEFT TO RIGHT *Green manures, such as Russian comfrey (left), red clover (center), and mustard (right), not only are an effective method of retaining and recycling nutrients in the soil, but act as ground cover, which prevents weeds from germinating.*

ABOVE *Fertilizers come in many shapes, forms, and sizes. The more concentrated they are, the greater the chance of their damaging, rather than benefiting, plants if they are not applied carefully.*

Fertilizers

Fertilizers can be either organic, of animal or plant origin, or inorganic, of mineral sources (see chart below). Plants can only use nutrients when these are dissolved in water. They do not actually feed, they drink, and many of the organic fertilizers, such as bone meal, are not readily soluble in water.

The smaller the fertilizer particles, the faster they are released into the soil. Nutrient release is dependent on the activity of soil-borne organisms, and in cold weather, when they are not so active, nutrient release is slower.

SLOW-RELEASE FERTILIZERS   These can be either organic or inorganic, and break down very slowly—some have a nutrient release period of years.

CONTROLLED-RELEASE FERTILIZERS   These are pellets containing a mixture of plant nutrients coated with a wax or resin compound, which has pores, or openings, on the surface. As water is attracted into the pellet, the fertilizer slowly dissolves and is released into the soil. This release can take place over a 6- to 18-month period, depending on the size and number of pores in the outer coating, soil moisture, temperature, and pH.

LIQUID FERTILIZERS AND MANURES   In many cases, liquid fertilizers are easier to apply than powder or granular formulations, and there are many brands of concentrated manure available. They are often safer to apply, since the distribution is easier and the plant's response can be very rapid. The concentrate can be either a liquid or a water-soluble powder. The fertilizer must be mixed thoroughly with the correct amount of water before applying

NITROGENOUS FERTILIZERS					
Fertilizer	% Nutrient			Type	Action
	N	P	K		
Ammonium nitrate	34			inorganic	fast
Ammonium sulfate	21			inorganic	fast
Basic slag		14		inorganic	slow
Bone meal	5	24		organic	slow
Dried blood	12			organic	fairly fast
Hoof and horn	12			organic	slow
Muriate of potash			60	inorganic	fast
Nitrate of potash	13		44	inorganic	fast
Nitrate of soda	16			inorganic	fast
Urea	46			inorganic	fast

it, in order to reduce the chance of damaging the plants. Avoid applying these fertilizers when rain is forecast, as they may be washed through the soil away from the plant's roots.

FOLIAR FOOD These are highly soluble nutrients applied as a solution to a plant's leaves. They are quickly absorbed by the leaves, work rapidly, and can be directed to specific areas of the plant.

This type of application is useful for plants with damaged roots or when the soil is very dry. It can also be applied as remedial food to overcome nutrient deficiencies. Ideally, these fertilizers should be applied early in the day or during cloudy conditions to avoid leaf scorch.

DISADVANTAGES OF CONCENTRATED INORGANIC FERTILIZERS

• Increasing the quantity of one nutrient can increase the demand for other nutrients by the plants, leading to a depletion in the soil.

• Fertilizers do not provide bulky organic matter and so are no substitute for manures such as farmyard manure.

• Overdoses may lead to toxic effects, for example, scorching, if dropped on foliage (more likely with inorganic fertilizers).

• The addition of one nutrient may decrease the uptake of another.

• Overuse can lead to environmental problems. High levels of nitrogen fertilizers have caused damage to lakes, streams, reservoirs, and rivers.

• The use of fertilizers without organic matter can lead to a loss of soil structure and soil erosion, and does not help retain or improve soil fertility.

testing soil pH

Most soils contain some free lime, and the presence of this lime (or lack of it) will cause the soil to be either "acid" or "alkaline," depending on the amount present. The lime content within the soil will greatly influence the range of plants that can be grown, as well as the overall fertility of the soil, so it is important to find out the pH value before adding plants to it. Many plants will grow happily in a soil with a high lime content, but there are others that cannot tolerate it and will die. Testing the soil will therefore save costly mistakes—both in terms of time and money.

There are a number of very easy-to-use soil testing kits available that evaluate a sample of soil taken from the garden as either acid or alkaline. If possible, take a soil sample every 12 sq. yds., and from the top 6 in. of soil. If a reading is required from a deeper level in the soil, make sure to keep the soil samples from different depths separate from one another in different bags. This is because the soil close to the surface is usually slightly more acidic than the soil from lower down in the ground, and mixing the samples may give a slightly inaccurate reading when it is tested.

For the most accurate reading, the test must be carried out on soil that is moist but not wet. It is very important to allow enough time for the sample to settle, and then you can compare the color against the chart. Samples that have a high proportion of clay will usually take longer to settle and clear, because the very fine soil particles in clay are held in suspension for longer.

AUTHOR'S TIP:
Storing chemicals

Store the chemicals from the soil testing kit in a cool, dark place; they may deteriorate if exposed to sunlight for long periods.

CLOCKWISE FROM TOP LEFT

Start by collecting a sample of moist soil using a trowel or spade, and place it in a plastic bag.

Pour the soil sample out of the bag and onto a sheet of absorbent paper. This will help to draw moisture out of the soil if it is very wet.

Using the back of the trowel, crush the soil sample lightly in order to break down any large lumps. Remove any large stones and discard them.

Using a test tube from a testing kit, add a measured amount of test chemical before adding a measured amount of soil from the sample into the tube.

Add distilled water up to the level indicated on the tube. Seal the top of the tube with either a cap or cork, and shake the contents vigorously for about one minute. Allow the solution to settle and clear. The liquid will gradually change color, indicating the amount of lime in the soil sample.

Check the color of the liquid in the test tube against the color codes on the pH indicator card. This will give you a reasonably accurate reading of the lime content of your soil.

TOOLS FOR THE JOB

1 trowel or spade

1 pH testing kit (one that includes a test tube with a cork or cap, test chemical, and a pH indicator card)

MATERIALS

1 plastic bag

1 sheet of absorbent paper

Distilled water

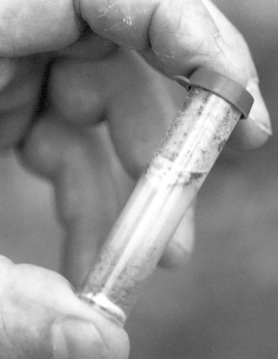

making leaf mold

Leaf mold is one of the most valued sources of organic matter a gardener can use. It makes an excellent soil conditioner, but it also has low levels of nutrients (0.4 percent nitrogen, 0.2 percent phosphate, and 0.3 percent potash), and is usually slightly acidic.

Leaf mold is a material that would slowly form naturally beneath trees in a woodland setting over many years, and making your own is a long-term project, because the leaves take time (up to two years) to decay into a dark, coarse and crumbly compost-like material. Fallen leaves from any deciduous trees and shrubs will eventually make leaf mold, although leaves of different species decay at different rates. The breakdown is slow because it is a cool process (unlike composting, which needs to be hot), and most of the decay is actually caused by the activity of fungi rather than bacteria.

For large gardens, the traditional method of making leaf mold is to have wire-sided composters that hold the leaves as they decompose. This system is best for large areas, where a new bin or pen is added each year, in order to have at least two of them in use.

Since the average garden is small, it may be difficult to find room to make leaf mold, but it is not impossible. Plastic bags, such as old potting compost bags, trash bags, or fertilizer bags, make good alternative containers for bins or pens, and they can be stored in any extra space around the garden.

AUTHOR'S TIP:
Accelerating leaf decay

To collect leaves from the lawn in a quick and easy way, run the lawnmower over them with the grass catcher attached. This will not only gather up most of the leaves, but it will also chop them up, accelerating their decay.

CLOCKWISE FROM TOP LEFT

Rake up the fallen leaves into piles. The best time to do this is just after it has rained, when the leaves are moist, but they can also be collected dry and watered later.

Make sure to remove any foreign material, such as plastic wrappers, from the piles.

Collect the leaves and place them in clear or black plastic bags. The latter are better—they block out most of the light and encourage fungal activity.

To every 1-ft. layer of leaves, add a small amount of organic fertilizer, such as dried, pelleted chicken manure or a measure of organic nitrogenous fertilizer, such as sulfate of ammonia (which contains 16–21 percent nitrogen).

When the bag is almost full, place it in the position where it is to be left while its contents decompose, and water it thoroughly so that the contents are soaking wet.

Over a period of about two years, the leaves will decompose and settle in the bag. These leaves will be pressed tightly together, with some remaining almost whole and others disintegrating completely. When the leaves are ready for use, the bag can be split open and the leaves used either as a mulch or soil conditioner.

TOOLS FOR THE JOB

1 rake

1 garden fork (optional)

1 watering can

MATERIALS

Black or clear plastic bags

Organic fertilizer

the deep bed system

Organic growing systems aim to reduce the amount of soil cultivation in order to preserve natural fertility and soil structure. Materials such as manure and other organic fertilizers are crucial to organic growing practices, since they help to build and maintain a good soil structure.

When using the deep bed system, the soil structure is improved to the required depth with one thorough cultivation, combined with the incorporation of large quantities of organic matter. From this point on, deep cultivations are kept to a bare minimum so that a natural soil structure develops and remains largely intact, and walking on the soil beds is avoided in order to prevent disturbance or compaction.

Very often the only cultivation that takes place once the bed has been established is either digging shallow planting holes to transplant seedlings of the next crop or digging up root vegetables when they are harvested. With

more organic matter added only as mulches and top dressings, it is quickly incorporated by the high worm population, allowing a natural soil structure to develop.

To achieve optimum results with a deep bed system, the soil must be loose and deeply dug, so roots can penetrate to the required depth rather than spreading sideways. The soil must also be enriched with plenty of organic matter like compost or manure. To reduce pest and disease problems, crop residue should be removed and composted in a separate area before being returned to the deep bed area later.

AUTHOR'S TIP:
Adding organic matter

On poorly drained ground, the top layer of soil can be forked over and the organic matter incorporated afterward. This process of adding more organic matter onto the surface can be repeated, but with no cultivation taking place.

CLOCKWISE FROM TOP LEFT

Mark one edge of the bed with a guideline. Measure 4 ft. across with a planting board and set up another guideline parallel to the first. Using canes, mark a trench 2 ft. wide; dig it out one spade deep, and keep the soil to fill the last trench.

Break up the exposed subsoil in the bottom of the trench with a fork, so roots penetrate deeply.

Put a 2–3-in. layer of well-rotted manure into the bottom of the trench to enrich the soil.

Leaving a cane in the corner of the first trench, measure another 2-ft. section with the other cane, so it contains the same amount of soil. Dig the soil and transfer it into the first trench, spreading it to cover the manure.

Add another 2–3-in. layer of manure into the first trench. The bulk of the manure and the loosened soil will raise the bed in height. Continue to dig out soil from the second trench and cover the new layer of manure, leaving a deep bed of loose, organically enriched soil in the first trench.

Scrape the soil from the bottom of the second trench. Break up the exposed soil. Repeat the steps until the whole plot is cultivated. Use the saved soil to cover the manure in the final trench.

TOOLS FOR THE JOB

Guidelines

1 planting board

1 spade

1 fork

1 wheelbarrow

MATERIALS

Canes or stakes

Manure

layering

This is an ideal method of propagation for the inexperienced gardener or someone who has a very expensive plant or a plant that is difficult to grow from cuttings. This is because there is no risk involved, since the young plant is separated from the parent only after it has formed roots and is growing independently. This technique enables fewer, but larger, plants to be produced—rather than a large number of small ones—which may suit the gardener better.

Layering is used mainly for woody plants and climbers, and the best times to carry it out are early spring, before growth actually begins, or summer, when the new season's growth is ripening. There are two main layering techniques: simple layering and tip layering.

Simple layering, as the name suggests, is one of the basic forms of layering, where soft, flexible shoots are bent down to reach the soil, and a section of the stem is buried.

Tip layering is an ideal method for plants that have long, trailing stems or can produce roots at the growing point (tip) of a shoot. It is frequently used as a means to propagate blackberries. If treated correctly, this tip will form roots and later produce a new shoot that, in turn, will emerge from the soil over a period of 6–8 weeks.

AUTHOR'S TIP:
Transplanting

Shoots can be rooted directly into pots of garden soil buried in the ground in order to make transplanting easier.

CLOCKWISE FROM TOP LEFT

Select a suitable shoot to be layered. At a point at least 1 ft. back from the tip of the shoot, make an angled cut (about 20 degrees) on the underside of the shoot using a knife. The cut should penetrate about one-third of the way through the shoot.

Dig a shallow hole in the ground and position the injured section of the shoot into the bottom of the hole.

Secure this shoot firmly into place with a wire hoop.

Replace the soil in the hole around the shoot and tamp the area well. Once the shoot has formed roots, sever the new plant from the old parent plant with a pruner. Leave it in position for another growing season before moving it to a new site.

In the summer, select one long, new, vigorous shoot and bend the tip down to soil level. Remove any leaves close to the tip using a pruner. Near the point where the stem touches the soil, dig a hole about 6 in. deep, and bury the tip of the shoot about 4 in. deep in the soil.

Tie the tip of the shoot to a short cane or stake in order to keep the young stem from moving.

TOOLS FOR THE JOB

1 knife

1 trowel

1 pruner

MATERIALS

1 wire hoop

String

1 short cane or stake

permaculture

This word first appeared in the 1970s and is now the accepted abbreviation of the original term "permanent agriculture." Permaculture is based on the concept of creating a natural growing environment that is both sustainable and self-sufficient—or getting as close to this as is practically possible.

Permaculture has evolved and developed over time into a whole philosophy of life for some people. In this specific context, it encompasses how to grow food, how to build energy-efficient housing, and how to create like-minded communities, all with minimal impact on the environment. For many, the most interesting part of the original concept is growing food using a form of sustainable agriculture and horticulture that has a minimal impact on the soil and nature. This involves working with nature as much as possible, rather than trying to create an alien system.

Many gardeners who choose to venture down what they interpret as the permaculture road are really looking at a form of organic cultivation that will involve trying to leave the soil in its natural state. In effect, they are considering a no-dig, or zero-cultivation, policy as a method of growing plants—particularly edible crops—although some digging may be required initially to plant deep-rooted subjects such as trees and shrubs.

A soil need not be cultivated to be well-drained and fertile. As a matter of fact, digging (or similar cultivation) can actually disrupt natural drainage, damage soil structure, and reduce organic matter content within the soil. In

ABOVE *Frogs and toads are definitely the gardener's friends. They live wherever the conditions are suitable and will devour slugs.*

BELOW *Cottage garden-style planting uses natural plant competition to control weeds by denying them space, light, and water.*

addition, a lack of soil disturbance can serve as the basis of a control for certain types of weeds that need the soil to be cultivated to germinate.

Leaving the soil uncultivated will not only reduce structural damage but will encourage the activities of beneficial soil organisms like worms and bacteria, by leaving them to develop natural colonies. These organisms can be further encouraged by planned, regular applications of organic matter, added to the surface as a mulch layer, which will then be gradually incorporated into the soil by these, and other, organisms. This activity works as the substitute for digging, because, as the organic matter is incorporated into the soil, it creates channels and air pockets that improve aeration and drainage without damaging the physical structure of the soil.

Fertilizers can still be used in this alternative system, but the organic mulch should be removed first, the fertilizers applied to the soil surface, and the mulch relaid afterward. Gardeners who adopt this system of growing tend to prefer organic rather than inorganic fertilizers. The layer of organic matter should be 3–4 in. deep to retain soil moisture and block out light, thus preventing the germination of weed seeds.

When seeds are sown or plants transplanted, the mulch is cleared away to expose the soil surface. For transplanting, the mulch can be replaced immediately. For seed sowing, the mulch should not cover the seeds but it can be gradually relaid around the emerging seedlings.

For crops like potatoes, instead of being earthed up with soil, additional layers of mulch are applied to raise the level around the plants, making them easier to harvest by simply pulling the mulch away. With this system, any crop roots that are not edible are left in the soil as a source of organic matter and also to improve drainage.

ABOVE *Plants grown in beds or blocks are easier to manage. Weed emergence is reduced and so is the need for cultivations.*

BELOW LEFT *Potatoes are an ideal "cleaning" crop, because earthing them up regularly kills off weed seedlings.*

BELOW RIGHT *A selection of clean, healthy potato tubers are left in the open for a few hours to allow their skins to toughen.*

new
BEGINNINGS

Once the new season gets under way and the plants start to grow, it is crucial to ensure that they keep growing, whether they are new plants from seeds or cuttings, or established plants regrowing after a period of imposed winter rest. Any check in the growth pattern of a plant will affect its performance, and this is why pricking out seedlings, potting cuttings, or transplanting young plants is such a critical stage for the plants concerned.

Professional plant producers and gardeners refer to this temporary halt in growth as "transplanting check" because they appreciate just how important and potentially dangerous this stage is. It is absolutely essential that plants that have just been moved be given extra care and attention to make sure that they recover from the trauma of the move, adapt to their new surroundings, and start to grow and establish.

Root disturbance, in particular, can slow down a plant's growth and leave it quite vulnerable to attack from pests and diseases. Some plants will react differently and "bolt" (flower prematurely), which can be disastrous for many vegetables, as well as annual and biennial flowers. During the first season after transplanting, woody plants such as trees, shrubs, fruit trees, and bushes, may only grow to one-third of the size of similar plants that have not been moved. Although this might worry an inexperienced gardener slightly, it is quite natural and often indicates that the plant is producing a large amount of new root growth, which will serve to support the leaf and shoot growth in subsequent years. In fact, some gardeners actually prevent plants from flowering or producing fruit during their maiden year.

At this stage, helping new plants establish as quickly as possible is crucial. The development of a good root system and a well-balanced framework of shoots and branches will go a long way toward establishing strong, sturdy plants that are self-reliant and perform well through the growing season.

RIGHT *Once spring gets under way, the plants seem to grow by the minute, with shoots and stems growing rapidly, and young leaves unfurling before your eyes.*

early days

If there is one time of the year a gardener really treasures, it is spring, when he or she can enjoy the very first rewards of the previous year's labors. The emergence of new shoots and leaves or, even better, flowers opening, will help to convince everyone that the winter is finally over and summer is on its way. Of course it is never quite that simple, and there will still be cold days and overnight frosts, but the days are getting longer and things are starting to happen—the garden has awakened.

ABOVE *Growing some bulbs in containers will brighten up a deck or patio with an early display of color before the plants in the garden are ready to flower.*

RIGHT *Tulips are one of the main flowers associated with spring. Their long, slender stems and bright, cheerful flowers particularly emphasize the sudden emergence of spring in the garden.*

Lifting and planting bulbs

Although they are actually a form of herbaceous perennial, bulbs are often placed in separate categories. Their grouping is broad and tends also to include other plants such as corms, rhizomes, and tubers.

Bulbs grown in the average garden have usually been propagated in North America, but may have originated in Europe, South Africa, the Mediterranean, or the Middle East. A careful selection of different forms and species enables you to have bulbs flowering any time through the year.

PLANTING DEPTH   Depending on the bulbs, planting depth can vary from as shallow as $\frac{1}{2}$ in. to a depth of 10 in. The depth is important since uneven planting leads to uneven flowering. This can spoil the effect of a mass grouping of bulbs, but can also be used to a gardener's advantage—by planting the bulbs slightly deeper, flowering can be delayed by up to 10 days. This way, planting half of the bulbs at the correct depth and the other half slightly deeper can extend the flowering display of each cultivar.

"LIFTING" AND STORAGE Bulbs are "lifted," or dug up, from the ground and stored for three main reasons: to make room in the beds and borders for other plants, because they are not hardy enough to overwinter outdoors, or because they are so congested their flowering performance is in decline.

Ideally, spring-flowering bulbs, such as hyacinths, narcissuses, and tulips, should be left in place until the foliage has died off. After the leaves have withered and died, carefully dig up the bulbs and allow them to dry for a week before carefully removing the dead leaves, roots, and old, shriveled skins. Place the cleaned bulbs, uncovered, in single layers in shallow boxes, and store them in a cool, dry place until ready for replanting in autumn. Any bulblets attached to the mother bulb can be used for propagation or discarded if not required.

In the mildest areas, gladiolus and dahlia tubers can be left undisturbed in the ground throughout the year, but elsewhere they should be lifted as soon as the first frosts begin. After lifting, cut down the top stems and leaves to about 6 in., and allow them to dry in a cool but frost-free place. Remove the stems and place the cleaned plants in single layers in shallow boxes then store them, uncovered, in a cool, dry place until they are ready to be replanted.

Overgrown clumps of hardy bulbs can be lifted at any time between midsummer and late summer, before being split up and replanted immediately. Congested clumps of snowdrops should be divided immediately after flowering in March, while they are still in leaf.

Where bed space is needed for summer plants, the bulbs can be dug up and "heeled-in" to a shallow trench on an unused piece of ground where they will complete their growing season and then die down.

Growing annuals and biennials

Hardy annuals and biennials are versatile and underrated. They can be propagated easily by sowing seeds outdoors in spring for an early, colorful display. Individual flowers may lack the beauty of more exotic specimens, but will provide broad swaths of vivid color throughout the summer. Take the time to deadhead the flowers as they finish, which will prevent seeds from forming and will allow a second, smaller display of flowers.

Raising hardy annuals early by sowing them under protection, in either a greenhouse or cold frame, will further extend the flowering season. Be sure that you grow them in shallow pots and then plant them out as young plants.

To provide even greater interest in your garden, mix annual seeds before sowing for a "cottage garden" effect. If sowings are repeated at two-week intervals in spring and early summer, they will flower well into the autumn.

ABOVE *Deadheading flowers may seem a chore but it really is the perfect way to keep plants neat and encourage them to continue flowering for as long as possible.*

ANNUALS AND BIENNIALS FOR SPRING SOWING	
Agrostis nebulosa	*Briza maxima*
Alcea rosea	*Campanula medium*
Campanula medium 'Calycanthema'	*Dianthus barbatus*
Eschscholzia californica	*Gypsophila elegans*
Hordeum jubatum	*Lavatera trimestris*
Lunaria annua	*Matthiola incana*
Pennisetum alopecuroides	*Setaria glauca*
Tricholaena rosea	*Zea japonica*

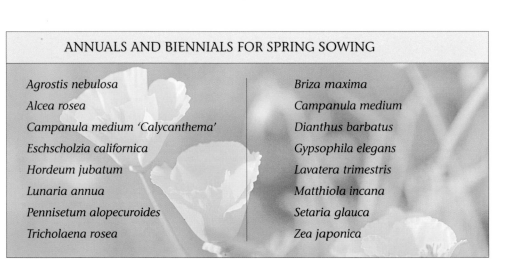

BELOW *Annuals are the perfect plants for providing broad swaths of color, and left to their own devices they will do their utmost to produce more flowers than their neighbors.*

Many annuals and biennials are capable of self-seeding and will reappear in the same spot, or close by, for a number of years after the initial sowings or plantings have been made.

HARDENING OFF Both seedlings and cuttings raised under protection will need to be toughened up for about two weeks in order to prepare them for transplanting outdoors into their permanent growing site. This can be done by moving the plants from the greenhouse into a cold frame or cloches, or by taking them out of the greenhouse for a couple of hours each day for progressively longer periods.

Perennials

Herbaceous perennials can be lifted, divided, and transplanted, either when they are dormant or, in the case of plants such as *Iris germanica*, during the growing season immediately after flowering.

Some plants should really be planted only in the spring and early summer. Plants in this category tend to have hollow stems or hairy leaves. Those with hollow stems are prone to getting rainwater trapped within the open end of the stem, causing the stem to rot at the base. Rot that starts in this way may well spread into the remainder of the plant. Plants with a hairy coating on the leaves and stems can trap water between the hairs, which again may lead to rotting. Planting as the weather conditions become drier gives plants like these the best chance of survival.

Perennials must be planted at the correct depth. Subjects, such as asters, with fibrous root systems, should have their roots just below the soil's surface, while those like acanthus, which have thick fleshy roots, or hostas, which produce a crown of buds, should be at least $^3/_4$–$1^1/_4$ in. below soil level.

Plants can be bought as either bare root or container-grown, but with herbaceous perennials, which produce soft, fleshy growth, it is important to water them well after planting and check them on a regular basis to prevent them from drying out.

ABOVE *Plants grown for sale in containers are very convenient for the gardener. They can be transplanted at any time of year and are ideal for providing an instant effect.*

BELOW *Container-grown plants with a healthy, fibrous root system will establish quickly when transplanted into a permanent growing position.*

HERBACEOUS PLANTS

With hollow stems		With hairy foliage	
Anchusa	Delphinium	Aster amellus	Anaphalis
Euphorbia	Kniphofia	Brunnera	Gaillardia
Liatris	Ligularia	Lychnis	Nepeta
Nerine	Papaver	Pulmonaria	Pyrethrum
Phlox	Sedum	Stachys	Symphytum

Vegetables

Spring and summer are periods of great activity in the vegetable garden but, as with any other time of the year, both ends of the cropping cycle can be seen as overwintered crops are harvested. Brussels sprouts, cabbages, and kale are among the vegetables that can be harvested fresh and eaten, but as soon as crops are finished, they must be cleared and composted quickly because they may have been overwintering sites for pests and diseases.

The main activity in spring is seed-sowing, when a wide range of plants are being raised for future crops. Most vegetables can be sown directly into well-prepared beds and thinned out to the appropriate spacing when the first true leaf has developed. Others, such as cucumbers, eggplant, peppers, and tomatoes, must start under protection, since the soil is too cold for them to germinate outdoors and they risk being damaged by late spring frosts. They are hence planted in early summer when they are 1–1½ ft. high.

THINNING SEEDLINGS Vegetables raised and grown in seedbeds in the garden are sown thinly into shallow seed drills in the spring and early summer. As the seeds and young seedlings are exposed to an unprotected environment, it is common to sow about 25 percent more seed to allow for potential losses. This means that once germinated, the seedlings will need to be given more room by removing some seedlings (thinning out) to allow enough room for the remaining seedlings to grow.

TRANSPLANTING SEEDLINGS With some crops, such as leeks, seedlings are grown until they are large enough to handle, and are then dug out of the seedbed and transplanted. Water the plants several hours before digging them up, so they have a reserve of water immediately after the move. To avoid injury to the roots, use a garden fork to dig up the plants, and hold them by their leaves and stems to prevent damaging the delicate root hairs.

ABOVE *The stout growth of curly-leaved kale, topped by its tightly bunched leaves, give it the appearance of a miniature tree.*

BELOW *Well-spaced seedlings will establish and grow very quickly because of the lack of competition during the critical, early stages of their growth.*

TRANSPLANTING PLANTS

Transplanting	Row width	Plant spacing
Cauliflower (early summer)	1½ ft.	2 ft.
Cauliflower (summer)	1½ ft.	2 ft.
Celery	1½ ft.	1½ ft.
Garlic	8 in.	8 in.
Onion sets	8 in.	6 in.
Potatoes	1¾ ft.	1 ft.

RAISING NEW PLANTS

Seed sowing	Row width	Plant spacing
Beet	1 ft.	4 ft.
Broccoli	40 seeds per tray sown indoors	
Brussels sprouts	40 seeds per tray sown indoors	
Cabbage, sum/aut	1½ ft.	1 ft.
Cabbage, winter	1½ ft.	1½ ft.
Calabrese	2 ft.	1 ft.
Carrot	6 in.	4 in.
Cauliflower, summer	40 seeds per tray sown indoors	
Cauliflower, early aut	1 ft.	6 in.
Cauliflower, autumn	1 ft.	6 in.
Cauliflower, winter	1 ft.	6 in.
Cauliflower, spring	1 ft.	6 ft.
Celeriac	40 seeds per tray sown indoors	
Celery	40 seeds per tray sown indoors	
Cucumber (ridge)	1 seed per 3 in. pot sown indoors	
Eggplant	1 seed per 3 in. pot sown indoors	
Fava bean	1 ft.	9 ft.
Kale	2 ft.	1½ ft.
Kidney bean	1 ft.	6 in.
Kohlrabi	1 ft.	6 in.
Leeks	4 in.	1 in.
Lettuce	1 ft.	1 ft.
Onion, green	4 in.	2 in.
Onion, seed	1 ft.	4 in.
Parsnip	1 ft.	6 ft.
Peas	5 in.	5 in.
Peppers	1 seed per 3-in. pot sown indoors	
Radish	6 in.	1 in.
Rutabaga	1¼ ft.	9 in.
Squash	1 seed per 3-in. pot sown indoors	
String bean	1 ft.	3 in.
Sweet corn	1 seed per 3-in. pot sown indoors	
Tomato	1 seed per 3-in. pot sown indoors	
Turnip	1 ft.	6 in.

ABOVE *Zucchini is the perfect summer vegetable. The fruits can be eaten cooked or raw and the flowers are an ideal ingredient in salad dishes.*

BELOW *In order to produce carrots of good quality, with long straight roots, a deep and well-cultivated soil is essential. The results will make the effort worthwhile.*

ABOVE *Pot-grown roses are the perfect example of convenience plants. They can be planted when in full growth—or even when in flower.*

BELOW *Some plants, particularly broad-leaved evergreens and conifers, seem to be happier when they are moved and transplanted with their rootballs intact.*

Planting trees and shrubs

Planting trees and shrubs is an important and satisfying gardening activity. These are the longest-living plants and create the framework of the garden. To do these plants justice and enable them to make a long-term impact, soil preparation must be thorough.

Planting is now a year-round activity; plants in containers are easily available throughout the year, depending on how they are grown and packaged (although many will establish better when planted in spring). The three main types available are:

BARE-ROOT PLANTS These are only available for about five months of the year when the plants are dormant. They are light and easy to handle, due to a lack of soil around the roots, and are also easier to plant and stake, since their roots are visible.

CONTAINER-GROWN PLANTS These plants are available year round. Containers are ideal for moving and handling plants that resent root disturbance or suffer a transplanting check.

ROOT-BALLED PLANTS These are available for about six months of the year while the plants are dormant. The root ball is wrapped in burlap or a similar material. This method of transplanting is better for plants like conifers and broad-leaved evergreens, which resent having their roots dry.

Regardless of which type of plant is being transplanted, it is important that the soil is well cultivated and weed-free before planting can commence. The planting hole needs to be at least twice the diameter of the plant's root ball, to encourage the new roots to grow out from the root ball and into the surrounding soil. Throughout the first summer after planting, all the newly transplanted plants should be kept both well-watered and weed-free. Vigorous weeds that are growing around the base of a new plant while it is establishing can reduce its growth potential in the first year by 25 to 30 percent. For instance, an ornamental tree that is 8–10 ft. high will often need 4–5 gallons of water each week just to stay alive.

Restoration of fruit trees

Restoration pruning techniques can be used to rejuvenate old fruit trees that are neglected or overgrown, by restoring their health and productivity and keeping them at a manageable size. Fruit trees are restored in early spring so the plants can respond almost immediately when new growth starts.

ABOVE *Pears benefit from summer pruning to encourage both the development of fruit-producing spurs and regular crops.*

BELOW *Plums are versatile fruits; they not only can be eaten straight from the tree but also are delicious cooked or preserved.*

If the tree lacks vigor and is making very little new growth, the entire tree can be pruned at once, or the pruning process can be phased over a two- or three-year period. Start by cutting out dead, damaged, and diseased branches. Then cut out any crossed or badly positioned branches, particularly in the center. Try to leave branches spaced about 1½–3 ft. apart. Pruning will usually result in a large amount of strong vigorous growths being produced by the fruit tree.

During the midsummer to late summer period (when the new growths have produced a minimum of 22 to 23 new leaves) many of the shoots can be pruned back to five leaves. This summer pruning will stimulate the tree to develop flower buds on these shortened shoots for the next year, and these will eventually form fruiting spurs. Other shoots will be allowed to grow and form replacement branches to take the place of some of the oldest branches over the subsequent few years.

"Stone," or pitted, fruits, such as cherries, damsons, greengages, and plums, are pruned similarly, but usually complete branches or major sections of branches are removed to allow more room for replacement shoots to develop. Many stone fruits can be pruned in the winter months, but pruning is best done in the summer when there are fewer fungal spores around. This reduces the risk of any fungal infections, which may enter the tree through pruning wounds made in the winter. The main danger of these fungal infections is that they attack living tissue, and eventually kill the entire tree. There are no effective methods of controlling them once they are established in the tree.

making a strawberry table

If there is one fruit that has a close association with summer, it is the strawberry. The sweet aroma and distinctive flavor of its ripe fruit on a summer's day are unmistakable. Although the actual plants are easy to grow, strawberries are not the easiest of fruit to manage and producing a crop of good quality fruit is a true challenge.

The low, spreading trusses of fruit that spread over the ground are easily damaged and are also easy prey for fungi, insects, and slugs. The low growth pattern of strawberries means that the fruits are awkward to pick, they are close to the ground, and are often obscured by the plant's dense foliage. In order to overcome these difficulties, there is an increasing trend toward growing strawberries in containers, especially if these are placed above the ground, so that the fruits hang below the leaves and are easily seen. There is also less chance of the fruits being tainted by the soil or eaten by slugs with this method. This, in turn, is a good way of reducing the use of either sprays or baits in order to control pest and disease problems, which also reduces the risk of tainting the flavor of the fruit.

Once the plants have finished cropping, they can be lifted off the table (complete with the growing bag) and allowed to grow elsewhere in the garden until the following year. A new growing bag containing autumn-fruiting strawberries can be placed on the table ready for producing a crop later in the year.

AUTHOR'S TIP:
Plant longevity

Most plants and growing bags will produce a good crop for two consecutive years. After that time, both should be discarded and replaced.

CLOCKWISE FROM TOP LEFT

Start by measuring and cutting two pieces of lumber to exactly the same length as the growing bag you are using, and measure and cut two other pieces of lumber to exactly the same width as the bag.

Drill both ends of each of the long sections of lumber. Turn them on edge, and fix the long lengths and short lengths together to form a rectangle.

Cut four 2-ft. pieces of 3-in. x 2-in. lumber and fasten one to each corner of the frame in order to form the legs.

Cut a section of wire mesh to cover the area of the wooden rectangle, and staple the wire mesh to the edges.

Place the growing bag in the frame, and cut out the middle section on the top of the plastic cover. Next, place the strawberry plants into the growing-bag compost and water them well.

The strawberries will grow much better if the table is placed in a sunny, well-lighted area.

TOOLS FOR THE JOB

1 saw

1 electric drill

1 hammer

1 crowbar

1 pair of pliers

1 watering can

MATERIALS

Measuring tape

Lumber

1 growing bag

Screws

Wire mesh

Staples

Strawberry plants

making an herb globe

Hanging containers filled with plants are a very useful way of growing plants when space is at a premium, and they can be filled with a range of bright, cheery plants or edible vegetables and herbs. The most common type of hanging container is the hanging basket, which is usually made of heavy-gauge wire coated in plastic.

The planting compost is usually a personal choice; a loam-based compost is preferred by many, but it can be very heavy after watering, as it retains moisture well. Others favor loam-free composts, which are lighter, but tend to dry out very quickly and can be difficult to rewet. Both types of compost will usually only last for one season, and the moss can only be used once as well, but the hanging basket itself can be used for many years.

Fresh herbs are very popular for flavoring cooked foods and salads, and a small number can be grown on a windowsill or in pots on a patio or balcony. Where space is limited, it is possible to garden in the air by using hanging baskets—even two fastened together in order to form a ball or globe—that can then be hung in a small space. Provided there is plenty of light and the plants are kept well-watered, it is possible to grow a range of herbs and salad plants that have leaves and fruits that can be harvested on a regular basis.

AUTHOR'S TIP:
Hanging the globe

Make sure that you hang the globe at a height that is easy to reach when cutting herbs for cooking.

CLOCKWISE FROM TOP LEFT

Place one basket on top of a large empty plant pot. Line the lower half with a layer of sphagnum moss, and press it firmly against the wire mesh, before adding compost to the same level.

Insert the first layer of herbs by passing them (roots first) through the mesh, so that the roots are resting on the compost and the tops of the plants are hanging down the sides. Line the top half of the basket with moss and compost as before. Insert the next layer of herbs, and add compost until it is level with the rim.

Place a square of plywood over the top of the basket before turning it over to form a dome. Nail the basket rim to the plywood. Leave in a sheltered place and water regularly for two to three weeks. Prepare the second basket in the same way.

When the herbs are well rooted in the compost, place the domes on a flat surface and remove the nails. Place one dome upside down on top of an empty plant pot.

Remove the plywood and place the second dome on top of the first.

Slide out the plywood from the second dome and secure them together with plastic-coated wire. Attach hanging chains to the herb globe and hang it in position.

TOOLS FOR THE JOB

1 hammer

1 pair of pliers

MATERIALS

2 hanging baskets and chains

1 empty plant pot

Sphagnum moss

Herbs

Compost

Plywood

Nails

Plastic-coated wire

herb directory
People have used herbs for medicine, decoration, and flavoring for many years. Growing herbs on a windowsill, in a container, or in the garden where they are harvested and used fresh, makes them the healthiest convenience food.

HERB DESCRIPTIONS

HERBS	PLANT TYPES	USES	PROPAGATION	COMMENTS
Angelica	A tall, majestic biennial plant that prefers a moist soil in semishade.	The seeds, stems, and flowers can all be used either fresh, cooked, or preserved.	Increased by seed, often self-seeding.	This plant is equally at home in an herb or ornamental garden.
Basil	Annual, up to 14 in. high. Needs good drainage.	Leaves are used cooked or raw as a flavoring.	By seed.	Can be difficult to grow.
Bay	Evergreen shrub or small tree. Needs a sunny, sheltered, and moist site.	Leaves used in cooking or as a decoration.	Semiripe cuttings taken in late summer.	Leaves can be dried and stored.
Borage	A self-sowing annual preferring a light, well-drained soil and full sun.	Flowers and leaves can be used either fresh or preserved in cooked or salad dishes.	Propagation is by seed sown in the spring.	This plant is valued for use as a flavoring in low-salt diets.
Chervil	An annual plant that prefers a well-drained soil and semishade.	Leaves can be used fresh in cooked or salad dishes.	Propagation is by seed sown in the spring.	Certain preparations can be used to ease swelling and bruising.
Chives	Perennial bulb that grows in sunny but moist position.	Leaves eaten raw, cooked, or as a garnish. Flowers can be used in salads.	By seed.	Leaves can be stored dry or in ice cubes.
Cilantro	Grown as a half-hardy annual. Prefers a light, well-drained soil.	The leaves and seeds can be used in a range of cooked and salad dishes.	Propagation is by seed sown under protection in the spring.	This plant can be grown to deter aphids and spider mites.
Dill	An annual plant preferring a light, well-drained soil and full sun.	The seeds, stems, and flowers can all be used either fresh, cooked, or preserved.	Propagation is by seed sown in the spring.	Often used for pickling, this plant is also used to aid digestion.
Fennel	An herbaceous perennial that grows in full sun.	Leaves used in salads, soups, and with oily fish. Stems used in salads.	By seed.	An attractive plant for a border, but self-seeds very easily.
Hyssop	Low-growing woody perennial. Prefers full sun and good drainage.	The leaves and flowers can be used in cooked or salad dishes.	Propagation is by seed or semiripe cuttings.	Planted around cabbages, it can be used to ward off harmful butterflies.
Horseradish	Hardy perennial. Prefers sun and moist soil.	The root is used in sauces or grated into coleslaw for a fiery flavor.	By seed, division, or root cuttings.	Flavoring oils are volatile, so root is not cooked.

HERB DESCRIPTIONS

HERBS	PLANT TYPES	USES	PROPAGATION	COMMENTS
	Juniper An evergreen woody perennial that prefers a well-drained soil.	The ripe berries can be used as a flavoring.	Propagation is by seed or semiripe cuttings.	The berries are used to give gin its very distinctive flavor.
	Lovage A tall herbaceous perennial. Prefers moist soil and semishade.	The seeds, stems, and flowers can all be used either fresh, cooked, or preserved.	Propagation is by seed or division in the spring.	Can be used in dried flower arrangements.
	Marjoram/Oregano Hardy perennial. Prefers sunny, well-drained sites.	The leaves are used in many Italian dishes, or with eggs and cheese.	By seed. Also root or stem cuttings in spring/summer.	Leaves can be infused and used as a hair conditioner.
	Parsley Hardy biennial. Prefers sunny, sheltered sites.	Leaves can be used raw in salads or as a garnish.	By seed.	Leaves can be stored dried or in ice cubes.
	Rosemary Evergreen shrub. Prefers sunny, well-drained sites.	Its flowers are used in salads and the leaves in cooking lamb and pork.	Semiripe cuttings in summer or layering.	The stems make good skewers for kebabs and the leaves deter insects.
	Sage Evergreen shrub. Prefers a sunny, well-drained site.	Its leaves are used in cooking, and also as a medicinal infusion.	By seed. Semiripe cuttings in summer.	Its dried leaves can be scattered among clothes to discourage insects.
	Sorrel Hardy perennial. Needs a moist site and good light.	Leaves eaten either raw in salads or cooked like spinach.	Seed sown in spring or division in autumn.	Remove the flowers to ensure production of more leaves.
	Spearmint Low-growing herbaceous perennial that grows in a wide range of soils.	The leaves and stems can be used in cooked or salad dishes.	Propagation is by division.	This plant has a reputation as an insect and rodent repellent.
	Tarragon Hardy perennial. Prefers a sunny, sheltered site.	Used in sauces and vinegars; also with soups, eggs, and tomatoes.	Semiripe cuttings in summer.	Divide and replant every three years to keep plant growing well.
	Thyme Evergreen sub-shrub. Prefers a sunny, well-drained site.	Leaves used fresh or dried in cooking. Also used as a disinfectant or in a potpourri.	Semiripe cuttings in summer, division, or layering.	Flowers are highly attractive to bees.
	Winter Savory Woody perennial. Likes full sun and deep soil.	The leaves and flowers can be used in cooked or salad dishes.	Propagation is by seed or semiripe cuttings.	Often planted around vegetables because it repels insects.

plant
PROPAGATION

The propagation or production of new plants has to be one of the most interesting aspects of gardening. Watching the development of a new plant as it grows, and knowing that it is your own achievement, is an extremely satisfying and rewarding experience.

As with many other hobbies, experience leads to greater interest and you may be enticed by the challenge of using different, perhaps less common, methods of producing familiar plants. This might involve attempting to cultivate root cuttings or germinate seeds of plants reputed to be harder to propagate, or trying your hand at the propagation of plants that need a much higher level of care and attention to provide any chance of success.

The best part of this particular aspect of gardening is that it can be as simple or as complicated as you want to make it, depending on the type of plants to be multiplied. At one end of the spectrum, the most basic form of propagating plants is by cultivating a small patch of the garden and sowing seeds or inserting cuttings into the soil. For this, all you need is the soil and the plant material. For the more experienced practitioner, a small, heated, enclosed box with a thermostat to control the temperature can greatly increase the range of plants that can be propagated.

For both the professional and less experienced gardeners, the ultimate challenge is to graft two plants together with the aim of producing a suitable combination for use in the garden. There are records of budding and grafting going back to Roman times, where they joined several cultivars together on a single rootstock. Even today, these techniques are seen as an opportunity for any gardener to test their skills. Many gardeners find that once they have successfully tried one method of propagation, they are hooked and have to try various other techniques, as well.

RIGHT *Creating new plants from pieces of existing ones, or from seeds, can be a very effective, cheap, and satisfying way of filling the garden with plants you will appreciate.*

seed and vegetative propagation

A large number of plants can be multiplied either by using seed to grow new plants or by some form of vegetative propagation, by using cuttings. Most gardeners will particularly appreciate those types of plants that can be increased by both seed and vegetative means of propagation.

Seed propagation

Gardeners usually start propagating by growing annuals from seed, in order to raise bedding plants or homegrown tomatoes. But this is only the beginning, as the variety of plants that can be grown from seed is almost limitless.

GETTING THE SEED The first decision to make is whether you want to buy seeds or go out and collect your own. Collecting your own seeds has a number of advantages since you can collect the seed at exactly the right stage (absolutely essential for some plants), observe the plant at close quarters beforehand, select only the best seed from the strongest, healthiest plants, feel confident that seedlings from locally growing plants are likely to do well in your area, and swap with other gardeners to expand your range of plants.

However, collecting your own seeds can prove difficult and may involve climbing ladders, as well as competing with wildlife. If you believe these problems outweigh the benefits, perhaps you should buy the seeds. If more unusual or exotic plants are desired, this may be your only option.

SEED TREATMENTS The seeds of some plants need to be exposed to certain conditions before their dormant period can end and germination takes place. This is particularly true of woody perennial plants, and the process may involve a period of exposure to cold temperatures, or "stratification," in order to simulate a winter. To do this, the seed should first be mixed with moist sand, since it must remain moist for any chemical changes to take place on the inside. This mixture can then either be stored outdoors in a shaded area for a year or be placed in a refrigerator for several weeks. However, other treatments, such as leaving it a number of weeks at room temperature, may also be required to complete the process.

For many woody plants, one way of avoiding this type of seed treatment is to collect the seed while the fruits are only half ripe. The seed is then immediately sown outdoors, and a high proportion will often germinate the following spring.

BELOW *Some plants produce seed that is identical to the parent plant, but hybrids can give rise to a wide range of different offspring.*

ABOVE *Cloches are useful "minipropagators," for raising seed or cuttings, and once plants are established, the cloches can be moved to the next propagation site.*

SEED SOWING If only a few plants are required, or if the seeds are too tender to germinate outdoors in spring, they can be sown under protection in a greenhouse or cold frame. This encourages the seeds to germinate and grow quickly. As soon as the seedlings are large enough to handle, they can be transplanted into trays or potted individually to give them more room and keep them growing rapidly.

When a large number of plants are required, or the seeds are hardy enough to germinate outdoors in the spring, they can be sown in a seedbed outdoors in the autumn. Unfortunately, some woody subjects germinate very early in spring from autumn sowings, and unless these seedlings can be protected from frost, it is better to sow them in the spring.

Sowing procedures depend on the type of seed being sown. Fine seed is usually broadcast on the surface of the soil and then covered with a thin layer of fine soil or sharp sand, which is then gently tamped down. Larger seeds can be sown in a broadcast fashion, with the aim of keeping them 3–4 in. apart. These particular seedlings are not normally "thinned out," they are left to grow until the autumn when they should be dug up and transplanted with wider spacing or potted.

ABOVE *To catch most of the seed, collect seedheads just before they are fully ripe, and allow them to shed these seeds onto some sheets of paper.*

RIGHT *Some members of the lily genus form embryo bulbs (bulblets) on the stem just above a leaf joint. These can be taken off and used to produce new plants.*

seed and vegetative propagation ❀ 89

Vegetative propagation

The aim of vegetative propagation is to produce young plants that are identical to their parent. However, with some plants that have great difficulty producing seed, it is the only way of increasing plant numbers.

PLANTS FROM CUTTINGS A cutting is a section of an existing plant that is cut off and made to form roots of its own in order to live as a plant in its own right. The cutting will be identical to the parent plant, and many plants that have arisen from a single seedling or by a natural mutation can only be reproduced in this way. For a large number of roses, shrubs, and herbaceous perennials, and a limited number of trees, the simplest method of increasing the number of plants is by taking cuttings.

The keys to success include selecting the right type of cutting, choosing the correct time of year (the right stage of growth), and providing the best rooting environment for the cutting.

• Soft-wood cuttings: These are taken from the soft, sappy tips of shoots, anytime from late spring until midsummer, before they start to become woody. This type of cutting usually needs to be kept in constantly warm, humid conditions in a plastic bag or enclosed box.

ABOVE *Cut soft-wood cuttings early in the morning, when they are still cool and coated with dew and are less likely to wilt.*

BELOW *Rambling roses and many bush roses are propagated commercially by the technique of budding, but some can be propagated just as easily by taking hard-wood cuttings.*

• Semiripe cuttings: These are taken just as the current season's shoots start to harden at the base, either main stems or side shoots. Cuttings of deciduous plants are usually taken between midsummer and late summer, whereas broad-leaved evergreens, such as laurels and conifers, often root much better if taken in early autumn. This specific type of cutting usually needs to be kept in a cold frame or plastic tent in order to root, with the more difficult ones put aside in an enclosed box.

• Hard-wood cuttings: These cuttings are taken in autumn and winter from the previous season's growth, although timing can be less critical than with other types of cutting. However, rooting is often more successful with hard-wood cuttings taken in early autumn, when the soil is warmer. The cuttings can form roots within six to eight weeks.

ROOT HORMONES Some cuttings, such as fuchsia and willow, root very easily—but the cuttings that are more difficult to root may need some extra help. This additional help will usually come in the form of root hormones. Root hormones are actually man-made copies of the hormones that occur naturally in plants and that help to heal wounds and form roots. When used correctly, they help cuttings produce callus and adventitious roots, which will eventually become their own root system.

BULB SCALING This particular method is a variation on propagation by cuttings and is used for some bulbs, such as lily and fritillaria, which have modified leaves in the form of bulb scales. These scales can be used with the aim of producing new plants.

A bulb should be dug up in the autumn and the outer scales snapped off and placed in a plastic bag that is filled with moist peat or a similar absorbent material. The bag should then be closed, but not sealed, and the mixture placed in a warm, dark place. After a period of approximately two to three months, miniature bulbs will have started to form at the base of each individual scale, and these can be potted in compost and grown for two or three years before they start flowering. The gardener can remove up to 80 percent of the scales from the parent bulb and it will still flower the following year.

Most bulbs will increase their numbers by one form of natural division or another, but this process can be a very slow one. The advantage of using vegetative propagation techniques like bulb scaling is that the natural processes of division are harnessed by the gardener in order to increase the number of plants being produced.

ABOVE *Some plants will root most readily when they are propagated from very soft, sappy growth (known as soft-wood cuttings).*

BELOW *Synthetic root hormones can be used to promote rapid cell division at the base of a cutting. This will encourage healing and the development of new roots.*

DIVISION AND ROOT CUTTINGS This is one of the easiest methods of multiplying some plants, especially herbaceous perennials. In fact, a large number of perennials need to be divided regularly in order for them to grow well. The usual times for dividing plants are in the autumn or the spring, but it can also be undertaken at other times, usually after flowering. You can do this with *Iris germanica* (flag iris), for example, as long as the divisions are kept well-watered after having been transplanted.

The basic technique is very simple and involves lifting the clump from the ground and dividing it into separate portions before replanting. The center of the clump may be old and diseased; if so, it should be discarded. The outer parts of the clump are normally the youngest and healthiest, and these are the sections that should be reused.

If the clump is too large to lift, it can be split into smaller sections and these can then be lifted one by one. Large, compacted clumps can be split into more manageable pieces by using two forks pushed back-to-back into the clumps and then pried apart. Once the portions are of a manageable size, search for a natural dividing point before gripping each piece and pulling it apart with both hands.

A plant that is extremely tightly packed, or has a woody crown, may need cutting in half with an old knife (or even an old pruning saw) in order to break it up into sections. Keep breaking up the clump until it will divide no

LEFT *Snowdrops are unusual because their propagation is far more successful if they are divided and transplanted while the plants are actively growing rather than when they are in their dormant stage.*

further, keeping only the strongest and healthiest segments. In order to be able to produce a new plant, each division should have a growing point (usually dormant buds in autumn or spring) and some roots. If so, most of them will produce flowers the following year.

Washing the clump with a hose allows you to see how the plants are joined together and where the best points are to divide the clump.

BELOW *Some plants will produce copious quantities of seed, and one sowing of seed may produce self-sown seedlings for many years afterward.*

CUTTINGS FROM THE UNDERWORLD Some plants do not produce stems that are suitable for taking stem cuttings, and other plants with a low, flat, rosette pattern will usually only produce a flower stem. These plants can often be raised from small pieces of root cuttings, taken from midautumn until early spring. If the cuttings are taken after growth has started in the spring, they may lose a lot of sap ("bleed") and shrivel up.

Root cuttings are usually quite short, about 2 in. long. For plants with thick, fleshy, or woody roots, you should cut the part nearest to the middle core or crown of the plant using a flat cut across the root. The cut you then need to do at the opposite end should be a slanting cut. This is because these cuttings are inserted vertically, and it is important to ensure that they are inserted the right side up, or bottom first, into the compost. On the other hand, for plants with thin roots, the cuttings can be made with a flat cut at each end, because they are laid horizontally on the compost before covering, so there is no top or bottom.

Although root cuttings are usually associated with the propagation of herbaceous perennials, there are many trees, shrubs, and climbing plants that can also be increased by root cuttings.

LAYERING This is a form of vegetative propagation that occurs naturally. Self-layers of many plants develop as they form roots from stems that touch the soil. These natural layers are often found when working in the garden; for instance, blackberries bend their shoots down to the soil so that the shoot tips root, forming layers.

Other plants cannot help but form layers; for example, strawberries send out horizontal stems, and new plants form at modified leaf joints before they touch the ground to root and grow as independent plants.

A more planned way of layering plants can be used with a wide range of plants, particularly those that are very difficult to propagate from cuttings without having sophisticated facilities. The best time to layer most plants is in the autumn or early spring.

There are a number of different layering techniques, but the easiest by far is simple layering. This particular method of propagation involves digging a shallow hole close to the parent plant and bending down a young (one- to two-year-old) stem. The midsection of this stem is then laid into the hole, and the tip is allowed to grow upward. The stem is held in place just below the surface of the soil using a wire pin, bent like a hairpin, or a stone. In order to stimulate root formation, it may help to split the section of the stem that will be buried in the soil.

ABOVE *Some plants are difficult to propagate from cuttings unless very specialized facilities are available. In this situation, the safest method of propagation is layering.*

BELOW *Plants like dogwoods and willows will layer quite naturally, with the stems of these plants forming roots at any point that touches the ground.*

The period of time taken for a layer to produce roots varies considerably and in the case of some woody plants, it can take several years. Once roots have developed, and the layer is obviously growing as a plant in its own right, the stem joining the parent plant to the new plant can be severed, and the new plant dug up when it is dormant.

For greater flexibility, dig the hole as you would normally do, but place a pot of compost in the hole. Bend the stem down into the pot, so that the layer roots directly into the compost. This makes it much easier to move and transplant the new plant once it has been severed from its parent, and also means it can be done at any time of year.

Propagation by layering is the perfect choice for the inexperienced gardener. Even with the most expensive plants, you only remove a section from the parent plant *after* it has formed roots—definitely a "no-risk" method of propagation. Another advantage of layering is that it produces a few large plants rather than large numbers of very small ones, as cutting would.

DROPPING Very similar to layering is a propagation method known as "dropping," which can be used for a wide range of plants. It is particularly useful for low-growing plants with an open, straggly pattern. Some types of plants, such as heathers, carnations, and hebes, can easily be propagated using this dropping technique.

In the spring, just as the new growth starts, a mixture of soil, peat, and grit (or loam-based compost) is sprinkled into the center of the plant, so that only the end 2–2³/₄ in. of each stem is exposed. If this mound of soil is kept well-watered, the buried stems should produce new roots all summer, and these newly rooted stems can be transplanted in the autumn.

ABOVE LEFT *Blackberries and loganberries with long, arching stems will droop down to the ground, where the shoot tips will produce roots and form new plants.*

ABOVE RIGHT *The stems of strawberries grow out horizontally from the parent plant, and, at each leaf joint, new young plants (called "runners'") are produced.*

BELOW *Plants that are good at self-seeding will often provide a wide range of colors and varied flower sizes when the new batch of seed germinates during the following years.*

SEED VERSUS VEGETATIVE PLANT PROPAGATION

SEED (SEXUAL PROPAGATION)

ADVANTAGES

- A large number of plants can be produced.
- It is relatively cheap.
- Plants generally live a long time.
- Many diseases cannot be passed on by seed transmission.
- Mixture of genetic material gives rise to new forms—essential in breeding new plants.
- Hybrids are often very vigorous.
- Seedling plants have a root system that establishes well.
- No need for specialized propagation facilities.
- Seeds are easily transported.
- Large quantities of plant material can be stored in a relatively small area.
- Some plants are hard to produce vegetatively.
- Seed will remain alive (in correct storage) for several years.

DISADVANTAGES

- Seed quality can be very variable and depends upon the health of the parent plant.
- Seed collected from different areas may produce plants with variable characteristics.
- The plants may not be totally identical to their parents.
- Only species can be propagated in this way, not cultivars, which need to be propagated in a vegetative way.
- It can take a long time for plants to reach flowering and seed-bearing age.

VEGETATIVE (ASEXUAL PROPAGATION)

ADVANTAGES

- The offspring are identical to the parent.
- Plants often produce flowers at a much younger age.
- It is the only way to propagate some plants, sterile cultivars and variegated plants, for example.

DISADVANTAGES

- The propagation methods may be very complicated, requiring special skills.
- Some propagation methods can be quite labor-intensive.
- Specialized facilities may be required.
- It is generally more difficult to produce large numbers of plants.
- Diseases are often transmitted from the parent to the new plants.
- Plant material cannot be stored.

RIGHT *Some plants need the protection of an enclosed environment, while others prefer to grow outdoors once they are established.*

soft-wood cuttings

The soft wood is the most immature part of a stem, and during propagation, it is the most difficult kind of cutting to keep alive because it is growing very quickly and is then suddenly separated from its water supply—its roots. On the other hand, the younger and more immature the cutting, the greater will be its ability to develop roots and so propagate successfully.

Soft-wood cuttings can be taken in the spring and summer from the fast-growing tips of strong, healthy plants. It is important to collect the cuttings and work quickly as you prepare them and insert them into the compost, and then place them in a warm, humid environment. This will prevent them from drying out and reduce the chances of their dying. Also, a warm, humid atmosphere within the propagator will keep the soft plant tissue moist and turgid until the cuttings have formed roots and are capable of drawing up water from the compost.

Wherever possible, take cuttings only from strong, healthy plants, rejecting any cuttings that show obvious signs of pests or disease, since these will most probably infect the healthy cuttings while they are all growing so close together.

For cuttings that are difficult to root, you could try dipping them in root-hormone preparation. This may speed up the rooting process and help the plant to produce a better root system, but it cannot make a cutting produce root.

AUTHOR'S TIP:
Plant hormones

Plant hormones are produced at the very young tip of the cutting, and they help promote root development. If you find the cuttings are too long, always shorten them from the base and keep the shoot tip (and thus the hormones) intact.

CLOCKWISE FROM TOP LEFT

Collect the fast-growing tips from the stems of the selected plant in the early morning (while they are still full of moisture) and place them in a moist plastic bag. Store them somewhere cool and shady until you are ready to prepare the cuttings.

Fill a container with an open, free-draining cuttings compost and firm it gently by tapping the base of the container to settle the compost.

Prepare the cuttings by trimming the base of the stem to just below a node (leaf joint) if the cutting is more than 4 in. long, or trim the tail if the cutting was taken with a heel. Remove the leaves from the bottom third of each cutting.

Dip the cut surface at the base of the cutting in a root-hormone preparation, tapping off the excess.

Insert each cutting into the compost to just above its lowest leaves. Label the cuttings clearly with the name of the plant and the date when the cuttings were taken.

Water the cuttings and compost from above, then leave the cuttings in a warm and humid environment for 6–12 weeks.

TOOLS FOR THE JOB

1 pruner

1 watering can

1 pencil

MATERIALS

1 plastic bag

1 container

Compost

Root hormone

Labels

sowing seeds outdoors

For the maximum number of seeds to germinate successfully, the environment must be right. The soil making up the seedbed must be moist and firm, with a fine, crumbly texture that isn't too light and fluffy. It should not contain too many stones, because they will make it difficult to make a drill row, or shallow trench, to place the seeds in. The smaller the seeds to be sown, the finer the tilth of the seedbed should be.

The seeds may be sown and grown in situ, with some of the plants spending their entire life in the same spot. Others may be removed and transplanted elsewhere; this is usually referred to as "thinning." In the latter instance, seeds are usually sown in rows (drills).

It may be preferable to have a seedbed area that is only used for sowing and growing young plants, all of which will be removed and transplanted elsewhere when they are large enough to handle. For this method of raising plants, the seeds may be broadcast over an area of 5 sq. ft.

The limiting factor for seed sowing in the spring tends to be the temperature of the soil, as most seeds need a minimum soil temperature, below which they will not germinate. They may even rot if they are left in cold, damp soil for too long. Covering the seedbed with a plastic cloche, or row cover, for 10–14 days before sowing will help to make the soil warmer.

AUTHOR'S TIP:
Labeling

Write a label recording the plant's name and the date of sowing, and place the label at the beginning of the row.

CLOCKWISE FROM TOP LEFT

Rake over the area where the seeds are to be sown using a fine-tined rake in order to make a crumbly surface layer with a fine texture and also remove any large stones or clods.

Mark off the rows with a stake at each end, and stretch garden twine between them as a guide. Use the edge of a draw hoe or the end of a cane to make the seed drill. The depth of a drill will generally depend on the size of the seeds: the smaller they are, the shallower the drill.

Sow the seeds by placing them in the palm of your hand and dribbling them into the drill through the space between your thumb and forefinger. Make sure to sow evenly, but not too thinly, as it is far better to thin out the seedlings rather than have large gaps between the future plants. Or, you can sow small pinches at regular intervals. This method, called station sowing, is much less wasteful of seeds and makes thinning easier. The spacing of the stations depends on the type of plant—beet seeds are usually sown at stations about 4 in., then the plants are usually thinned 4–5 in. apart.

Cover the seeds by drawing the back of the fine-tined rake along the line of the drill. Then lightly tamp the soil with the back of the rake.

In order to have a record of what you have sown and where, insert a label at the end of each row of seed drill you create.

TOOLS FOR THE JOB

1 fine-tined rake

Guidelines

1 draw hoe or cane

1 pencil or marking pen

MATERIALS

Stakes

Seeds

Labels

propagating plants indoors

Growing plants from seed is a cheap way of increasing plant numbers. The joy of producing and nurturing new, young plants is also most rewarding. It is possible to produce a large number of plants in a small area, whether they are bedding plants, perennials, vegetables, or shrubs—from seed that has either been purchased or harvested from your own garden.

For most of these seeds to germinate quickly, they require a relatively warm, humid environment to begin with, but most will cope with cooler and drier growing conditions once germinated. Unfortunately, the warm, damp conditions initially required are also ideal conditions for the development and spread of plant pests and diseases, particularly fungal diseases. To avoid these problems it is important to always use either new containers or clean, disinfected seed

trays and pots, as well as a compost that has been sterilized (pasteurized). Ideally, the area where the seeds are placed to germinate should also be disinfected to reduce the risk of contamination.

The most common method used to propagate indoors is to sow a number of seeds into a pot or tray, and after germination to transplant the individual seedlings into larger trays or pots so they have more room to grow. However, some plants resent root disturbance and if the roots are damaged, the seedlings will often rot and die. To avoid this problem, the seeds of such plants are often sown individually into small separate pots.

AUTHOR'S TIP:
Watering seeds

To water seeds after sowing, start by pouring the water away from the container and, once an even flow is attained, direct it over the seeds. When you stop watering, move the water away from the container and stop the flow.

CLOCKWISE FROM TOP LEFT

Fill a seed tray with compost until it is heaped above the rim of the tray. Using a striking board, strike off the surplus compost with a sawing motion until it is level with the rim of the tray.

Using a presser board, firm the compost lightly to an even level that is just below the rim of the seed tray.

Sow the seeds evenly across the surface of the compost, making sure to keep your hand low to keep the seed from bouncing around too much.

Cover the seeds by sieving on compost, keeping the sieve low over the seeds. Label the seeds with their full name and the date of sowing.

Water the seeds from above, using a watering can with a fine nozzle. For fine seeds, it may be better to water from below by placing a shallow tray of water underneath the seed tray. Cover the seed tray with a sheet of glass to ensure that the seeds stay moist and warm.

Place a sheet of paper over the glass in order to minimize temperature fluctuations.

TOOLS FOR THE JOB

1 small striking board

1 presser board

1 sieve

1 pencil

1 watering can with a fine nozzle

MATERIALS

1 seed tray

Compost

Labels

1 sheet of glass

1 sheet of paper

seasonal
PRUNING

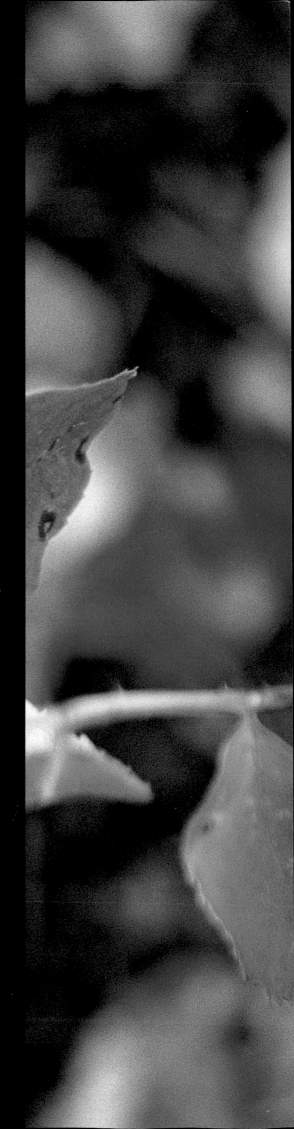

Pruning can be described as the removal of a part or parts of a plant by the gardener with a specific purpose in mind. At first glance, pruning appears to be a winter gardening job, when the soil is too wet to work, and burning the waste resulting from pruning offers warmth on a cold, frosty day. Unfortunately, winter is not necessarily the best time to prune from the plant's point of view.

Pruning is really a year-round task, and many plants will respond more positively if they are pruned while they are actively growing. Often, the fact that the plant is in full growth will make the gardener's job easier. For example, when removing dead wood from trees and shrubs, the dead and dying parts of the plant are much easier to spot and remove when the healthy growth is in full leaf.

Summer pruning of fruit trees and other woody plants has long been used to encourage them to develop flowers and fruit for the following season, and to help to suppress the excessive shoot growth that is often the result of winter pruning. A combination of summer pruning and training shoots to grow horizontally will make some plants much more productive; training shoots in this way causes a change in the plant's hormonal balance, stimulating greater flower and fruit development. Many ornamental plants benefit from being pruned immediately after they have finished flowering, because this will give the plant a whole year to recover and produce flowers for the following year.

Routine pruning operations, such as deadheading to remove dead and dying flowers, can be used to encourage flowering plants to keep producing flowers by not allowing them to develop seed until very late in the season. Even cutting and harvesting blooms for indoor displays may help to persuade the plants to continue producing flowers for a longer period.

RIGHT *Some flowering plants, such as roses, will flower even if they are not pruned at all. However, the flower's size and quality will be poor, and the overcrowded branches often harbor pests and diseases.*

reasons for pruning
Pruning is an important aspect of gardening because it enables you to manage and control the growth of a large number of plants. It is possible to prune the same plant at different stages of its development to achieve very different results. The reasons for pruning plants are numerous and varied. It may be done to train the plant; maintain plant health; obtain a smooth balance between the growth and flowering phases; improve the quality of flowers, fruit, foliage, or stems; or restrict growth and improve safety.

BELOW *Pruning is more beneficial to plants when the cuts are clean and neat with no bruising of the tissue. This enables the cuts to heal quickly, reducing the risk of infection.*

TRAINING For plants to grow in a desired shape or pattern some type of formative pruning may be necessary in order to persuade the plant to grow in a particular way. Building up an initial framework means it will be easier to manage the tree, shrub, or climber in later years. A plant of a required size and shape can be created that is not only well-balanced and good to look at but, in the case of fruit trees, carries flowers or fruits where they can be easily reached. In this way, pruning enables the gardener to make his garden setup more "user-friendly."

Although pruning in the early years of a plant's life delays flowering, it ensures a framework of strong, well-spaced branches that should produce flowers and fruit later. Left to grow naturally, many plants will start to flower earlier in their life, but this early flowering may actually be harmful to the plant's long-term existence.

MAINTAINING PLANT HEALTH Gardeners spend a great deal of time trying to control pests and diseases, and this can be achieved much more easily if the cause and conditions favorable to these afflictions can be removed or prevented as early as possible. Pruning is one way in which this can be done. Removing overcrowded growth allows the free movement of air and the entry of light into the center of the plant, which helps to discourage fungal attack and insect colonization.

In the early part of a plant's life, pests and diseases can retard growth and development, destroying flowers or fruit and weakening the stem and branch structure. Although some pests and diseases can be controlled by routine spraying of smaller plants, this becomes quite arduous (if not impossible) on large trees, so pruning is the most realistic method of control. Many diseases that attack woody plants enter through wounds and then spread throughout the plant, killing branches and stems, and eventually killing the plant altogether.

When diseased wood is being removed, always cut right back to the healthy wood. Dead wood on a plant is always unsightly and likely to break off, which will cause damage. It is also the main source for disease that can spread from the dead wood to the live (for example, coral fungus).

MAINTAINING A BALANCE BETWEEN GROWTH AND FLOWERING

With a large number of plants, once they have started to flower on a regular basis, shoot production will progressively decline until they reach their mature stage. At maturity, very little annual growth is added. Notably, in a mature plant, it is the young wood that produces the leaves as well as the flowers.

With age, both the quality of a plant's leaves and flowers and the rate at which these are produced decline. It is therefore desirable to encourage a woody plant to maintain the production of some young wood by regular pruning. Heavy pruning can stimulate the production of large quantities of leaf and shoot growth, which may subsequently delay or even prevent flowering for a number of years.

ABOVE *Diseases, such as brown rot, carry over from one year to the next. Affected fruit must be removed and burned to prevent propagation.*

BELOW *Vigorous plants, like vines and other climbers, need regular pruning to keep them within their allotted bounds.*

ABOVE *Some pests and diseases may do little actual damage to fruit, but these unsightly scars and blemishes make the fruit misshapen and unattractive to look at.*

IMPROVING QUALITY The greater the quantity of flowers and fruit produced by a plant, the smaller these individual flowers and fruits tend to become, as can be seen on any neglected shrub or fruit tree. Pruning reduces the amount of wood and so diverts energy into the production of larger, though fewer, flowers and/or fruits, and larger, healthier fruits usually keep better than small fruits. Even with some fruiting plants that are pruned regularly, there may be years when large quantities of small fruit are produced. Removing some of the fruit (which is known as "thinning") will allow those remaining to fully develop.

Some plants are grown for their attractive, colorful leaves, and these are mostly found on the newly developed growth. The more vigorous this growth is, the larger the leaves will be. Pruning plants that have colored leaves will produce more intense, richer coloring.

Certain deciduous shrubs are popular for their brightly colored bark. Their winter color is remarkable, especially on young stems. Dogwoods (*Cornus* spp.) and various willows are known for their brightly colored red, yellow, or orange stems. The greatest length and most intense color in these plants are usually the result of hard pruning.

ABOVE *Some pests seek shelter in plants with crowded branches and stems. Pruning to open up the growth will encourage birds and other predators of such pests to search for food.*

RIGHT *In wet summers, some pruning may be carried out during the growing season to slow down over-vigorous shoot growth and reduce the number of thin, weak shoots.*

ABOVE *Heavy crops of fruit can lead to large numbers of poor quality fruits being produced, and may even lead to a reduction in the number of fruits the tree is able to produce the following year.*

BELOW *Fungal diseases can survive the winter by living in twigs and buds. Pruning the infected areas can reduce the amount of disease that develops the following year.*

RESTRICTING GROWTH Plants left to grow and develop naturally will often continue to grow larger and larger. Unless they have unlimited room, they will gradually spread beyond their allotted space and so pruning becomes necessary to keep them within bounds.

REGULATING SAFETY Your garden should be not only aesthetically satisfying but also a safe haven. Safety regulation applies particularly to very large shrubs or trees whose branches (dead or live) overhang the street or sidewalk, and could possibly cause injury to passersby. In this case, some pruning may be necessary, even though the plant has no other requirement for it.

Pruning techniques

The first rule of pruning is to apply the "4-Ds Rule," which is the immediate removal of any plant material that is either dead, dying, diseased, or damaged. Only when this has been done is it possible to assess the potential of the remaining live, healthy stems and branches, and to develop a strategy for pruning this remaining growth.

The next stage is to remove any thin, weak, or straggly shoots, so that only healthy, usable shoots remain. The gardener can then decide which branches should be pruned back or removed to achieve well-balanced growth. It is very important to always try to work with the pattern of the plant rather than trying to prune in such a way that means you end up fighting its natural growth pattern.

RENEWAL PRUNING This is a method of pruning based upon a system of removing whole branches, or sections of branches, on a regular basis to encourage new shoots to develop as replacements for the branches that have been removed.

POSITIONING PRUNING CUTS Before pruning starts, it is essential to have a close look at how the buds are arranged. For plants where the buds are arranged alternately, any cut you make should be at an angle, $^1/_4$ in. above a bud, with the bud itself near the high point of the cut. This is important because wound healing is faster when the cut is close to the growth bud. The buds produce a hormone that stimulates the formation of healing tissue close by.

Plants that have buds arranged in opposite pairs are pruned by cutting at right angles to the stem just above a pair of buds but as close as possible without causing any damage to them.

ABOVE Some plants have their flowers harvested when fully open, particularly flowers destined to be dried and preserved.

BELOW Hard pruning some established plants can stimulate new growth, which can then be trimmed and reshaped to form "new" plants.

PRUNING WOUND TREATMENTS Whenever a pruning cut is made, there is always a risk of decay developing within the wound, gradually invading the plant, and ultimately killing it. Since Roman times, gardeners have been advised to cover pruning cuts in a misguided belief that wound dressings helped to protect the plant from infection.

More recently, research has begun to show that wound paints are not a very effective preventive measure for controlling diseases and, in some cases, may even encourage them by sealing the spores of infectious diseases into new wounds.

Numerous plants possess chemical and physical barriers that occur naturally within their tissue and that offer resistance to the invasion of rot-causing fungi. Pruning wounds, as with any other injuries a plant might suffer, creates possible entry points for disease, but the risk is reduced by making well-placed, clean cuts with sharp, well-maintained tools that are used quickly and skillfully.

ROOT PRUNING   This pruning technique is sometimes used as a method of controlling the vigor of trees and shrubs, as well as making them produce more flowers. Initially, this method subjects the plant to stress while the root wounds heal.

This technique is effective because certain chemicals that occur in the roots of plants actually influence the rate of growth and spread of the top growth and branches. By removing sections of root, the manufacture and supply of these chemicals are restricted, which in turn hinders the development and extension growth of the branches.

ABOVE   The summer pruning of young shoots can be used to encourage the formation of fruit buds that should lead to increased fruit production in coming years.

BELOW   Pruning thick branches should be carried out in stages to remove excess weight and reduce the risk of tears and splits in the main stem. Such splits disfigure the tree and provide a site for fungal infection.

Other forms of pruning

There are a number of alternative methods of pruning that will prove useful. One method is deadheading, which is the removal of the spent blooms from the plant. This may stimulate the development of another flush of flowers, and will prevent the formation of seeds. Once the plant starts to divert energy into forming seed, the tendency to produce flowers decreases, and eventually stops completely.

Pinching, or "stopping," is one of the main techniques used in shaping a plant. It involves the removal of the plant's growing point in order to encourage the side shoots to develop. The trimming of hedges is a perfect example of stopping.

Topiary is the clipping of bushes into unnatural shapes. It is a combination of training and restrictive pruning, like pleaching, which is used to make living screens or arches.

Another pruning method is harvesting, which consists of cutting flowers for indoor display.

Pruning can prove to be a delicate operation and therefore it is most important to have a clear idea of what is to be achieved well before the cutting actually starts.

formative pruning—the spindlebush

Formative pruning is used to shape a plant in order to help it construct a framework of stems and branches that will give it structural strength and stability. It is a process that may take several years before the desired shape and structure are achieved.

The spindlebush form of tree was developed for commercial fruit growers who wanted orchards with lots of small trees planted closely together. Trees are pruned to form a cone shape in order for all of the fruit to be exposed to sunlight for ripening, and also so they can easily be seen and picked.

To create a spindlebush, you must develop the three or four lowest branches so they become a cropping platform bearing most of the fruit. This is achieved by pruning those shoots that would otherwise develop in the center of the tree, spoiling the cone shape. A support stake may be needed but is only essential on light soils. The main cropping branches are tied down into a horizontal position in the summer. These horizontal shoots will produce more fruit than those growing into an upright position. Shoots that develop higher in the tree are allowed to produce fruit and are then pruned severely, to be replaced by fresh growth.

Select a tree with a straight stem and evenly spaced side branches radiating out from the main stem. These should be 2–3 ft. above soil level, and soon after planting, all other side branches below this level should be removed.

AUTHOR'S TIP:
Apple trees

For apples, it is recommended to select trees that are growing on dwarfing rootstocks, because this will help to control the vigor of the fruit tree in a considerable way.

CLOCKWISE FROM TOP LEFT

Toward the end of the summer, strong growths should be tied down into a horizontal position, in order to discourage shoot growth and encourage the tree to fruit. If the cultivar is a weak grower, tying is not necessary.

Tie down the lateral branches to a 30 degree angle with string secured to the base of the tree.

Remove very vigorous shoots that are growing upward from the main stem and any lateral shoots as well. Tie the main stem using staples hammered onto a support stake to keep it growing vertically.

As the tree develops, cut the main stem back by one-third of its original length, and remove the strings from the horizontal lateral branches (these branches will be "set" into position once the wood matures).

A new layer of branches can be tied into position, forming a second tier of horizontal branches. Those shoots not selected for tying down should be cut back to a single bud.

Repeat the above procedure in order to create a third tier of horizontal branches. Fruit will form on the lowest tier of horizontal branches.

TOOLS FOR THE JOB

1 pruner

1 hammer

MATERIALS

Strong string

Staples

1 support stake

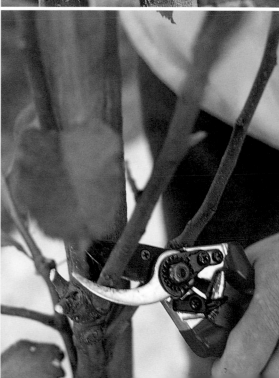

summer pruning of fruit

Once fruit trees are established and have developed a strong, well-formed framework of branches, the emphasis of pruning changes. The aim is then to get the tree to produce a constant supply of fruit buds, and also to limit any vigorous shoot growth. As winter pruning stimulates vigorous shoot growth in spring, most of this pruning is carried out in late summer, when young shoots are woody at the base and each shoot has formed over twenty leaves.

The whole basis of pruning at this time of year is to work within the plant's natural growth pattern to achieve the desired effect for the gardener's requirements. As a method of pruning, it can be used on many types of trees, but it is particularly useful on trained trees, including cordons, espaliers, and fans, as well as trees growing on the dwarfing rootstocks.

As the average garden is getting smaller, trees are being developed to match, with cropping varieties on dwarfing rootstocks. The aim for these trees is to bear as much fruit as possible, which makes this type of pruning increasingly popular.

Summer pruning is usually carried out only once each year. However, in a very wet summer, secondary growth may develop just below the pruning cuts, and a second, light prune, about a month to six weeks after the first pruning, will become necessary.

AUTHOR'S TIP:
Pitted-fruit trees

For pitted-fruit trees, such as plum or cherry trees, complete branches or sections of branches should be removed, leaving room for replacements to grow into the gaps created.

CLOCKWISE FROM TOP LEFT

Start by pruning any obvious signs of pests and disease and removing any dead or dying shoots; this keeps infection from spreading into the main branch framework.

When this is completed, cut back the main side branches to about three to five buds from the base of each shoot. Make sure the cuts are positioned about $1/4$ in. above the remaining top bud so that the cuts heal within a month.

Where several shoots emerge from a very similar place, remove the smaller ones completely, leaving only the strongest before pruning them back to five buds.

Shoots growing from spurs and existing smaller side branches can be pruned back to just one or two leaves above the base of each shoot.

Some fruit thinning may also be necessary at this time, so remove the smallest fruits by cutting through their stalks, but leave the larger fruits to develop and ripen.

Leave about ten percent of the longer shoots unpruned, but tie them to other branches so that they are roughly horizontal. This will draw the sap down, and discourage the development of any secondary growth.

TOOLS FOR THE JOB

1 pruner

MATERIALS

Strong string

budding

The technique of budding, or grafting, roses has been known for centuries, and, although many roses will produce new plants if propagated from cuttings, budding will produce a larger plant in a shorter time frame. To grow well, the plant requires a strong and vigorous root system but, unfortunately, many modern flowering roses either produce a poor root system of their own or refuse to produce roots at all.

Quite simply, budding involves grafting two separate but closely related plants together so that they appear to be a single plant. The aim is to use the root system from one plant to support the top growth of another. Although, in theory, any variety of rose can be budded onto another, the success or failure of this technique often depends on the availability of a suitable rootstock and its ability to accept a bud joined onto it. The bud concerned is the dormant eye of a cultivar that the gardener has decided to propagate. When it is transferred to a selected rootstock and inserted under its soft, sappy bark, the rootstock should provide the required growth and vigor to produce a strong, healthy rose plant.

For these two plants to be able to join, they must both be actively growing, so successful budding can only happen from early to late summer. However, the whole process from planting the rootstock through to producing a flowering rose plant from budding will actually take around one and a half years.

AUTHOR'S TIP:
Preventing budding failure

Do NOT touch the back of the bud; grease from your fingers will keep good contact from being made with the rootstock and a budding may fail.

CLOCKWISE FROM TOP LEFT

In midsummer, hoe away the earth from the neck of a one-year-old rootstock to expose it to air.

Make a T-shaped cut into the neck of the rootstock. Twist the knife gently to open the flaps of bark and expose the wood beneath.

Select a suitable rose cultivar with fully open flowers. Remove the growing tip, flowers, leaves, and thorns to leave a $\frac{1}{2}$-in. stub of leaf stalk. Remove the bud by shallowly cutting under it upward toward the tip of the stem. Lift the bud by holding ONLY the leaf stub.

Extract any wood from the back of the bud.

Holding the bud by the stub of leaf stalk, insert it, base first, downward, between the flaps of bark on the rootstock. Finally, trim off any surplus bark from the bud, flush with the horizontal cut.

Cover the bud with a rubber band, pressing it firmly, and pin it into position with a staple. In late winter, cut off the top of the rootstock just above the bud.

TOOLS FOR THE JOB

1 small hoe

1 sharp knife

1 pruner

MATERIALS

1 rose rootstock

1 bud stick

1 rubber band

1 staple

routine
MAINTENANCE

It is very satisfying for any gardener to produce plants from seeds and cuttings, because the results are both dramatic and rewarding. The real gardening skills tend to come later though, and may not bring such obvious rewards. Keeping your plants well fed and actively growing is essential in order to capitalize on a good start made with the initial growth of spring. All too often, plants seem to "run out of steam" during the season as growth slows, leaves look pale or stunted, and both flowers and fruits fail to reach their expected sizes. Plants will need regular observation in order to monitor their progress and rectify any problems before they have a chance to develop fully. This approach is all the more important for gardeners who are reluctant to use any chemicals. Primary fungal infections or insect infestations can be removed by hand as a means of reducing the chance of spreading a miniepidemic through the plants.

Plants need help in many ways in order for them to perform satisfactorily. This may involve a helping hand in terms of protection as well as feeding, to give plants an early start, or to keep marauding birds, animals, and insects away from fruits as they develop and start to ripen.

Other aspects of spring and summer gardening routines include: pruning, to shape and develop new young plants or to encourage better fruiting; deadheading, important for continued performance throughout the season; and frequent and efficient watering during the driest part of the growing season, which affects both the growth and the overall health of the plants.

The best approach to routine maintenance is one of "little and often" rather than leaving routine tasks, such as weed control or pruning, until they become major projects. Of course, there are other routine jobs, but many of them, such as the picking of the first strawberries of the season, don't actually seem like work at all.

RIGHT *A well laid-out garden with beds and borders of a manageable size always seems much easier to maintain and keep tidy, especially where the multiple paths are even and well defined.*

keeping plants growing

Although it may seem obvious that a gardener would want to keep his plants growing well, there is also a clear logic behind the objective. When plants are subjected to a slowing down of their growth, they tend to be much more vulnerable to attacks from pests and diseases, particularly if the check in growth is for a prolonged period of time.

ABOVE *Runner beans are a favorite garden vegetable. They are easy to grow, enjoyable to eat, and can grow in a confined space when trained up stake supports or cages.*

OPPOSITE PAGE *Cottage-style gardens are very popular not only because they are colorful but also because the semiwild approach of letting the plants grow into one another is a very effective method of smothering weeds.*

While it may be unsatisfactory to force plants to grow too rapidly and thus produce a lot of soft, sappy growth, it is important to keep plant growth progressing. Any incident in a plant's life that causes a slowing down or stoppage of growth puts that plant at risk. When seedlings or rooted cuttings are transplanted, it is crucial to care for them and do everything possible to reduce this risk of a "transplanting check." While plants that have just been repotted or transplanted are adapting to their new environment, they are in a most vulnerable condition, even if they have suffered little or no root damage or disturbance.

Providing shelter can increase a plant's growth potential by up to 30 percent, which is why hedges and screens are so vital within a garden. Tying and staking plants can also be essential factors in how well they will grow. For plants like roses, trees, and shrubs, staking is not necessarily to keep them growing upright but is used to keep the tops from rocking in the wind. This swaying movement would be transferred to the roots, and the tender new roots that are searching out into the soil are very easily broken by such movement transferred down from the stem.

The long stems of plants like climbers or wall shrubs will produce less extension growth if they are not supported by a framework. If these shoots are left untied and are allowed to whip about in the wind, they may become damaged or damage other shoots close by. Any damaged areas are then much more prone to attacks from pests and diseases.

One cause of stress to plants in the summer is water supply. There may be times when a plant will not have all of the water it requires and it may wilt, causing stress and a check in growth. Unfortunately, the common remedy for wilting plants is to give them a good soaking—but this will also expel most of the air from the soil or compost where the plant is growing, further stressing the plant due to the low level of oxygen it now has around the roots. Over a short time, perhaps only a few hours, the plant's available water levels will have fluctuated from a critical low point to a dangerous high point, with both extremes being equally dangerous for the plant's health.

ABOVE *For some plants, such as tomatoes, timing when to apply water in relation to the plant's development can be as critical as how much water is actually applied.*

BELOW *Obviously, some plants need more water than others. Clematis prefers cool, damp roots, as does dicentra, which has very soft, fleshy stems—very much like a succulent.*

Plants suffering from stress release chemical signals that can be detected by pests, such as sap-sucking insects, that become attracted to the ailing plant as a food source. The insects can cause even more damage.

Watering

Many plants produce their most rapid growth during the spring and summer, and some, such as vegetables, consist of up to 90 percent water. Large amounts of water are therefore required, since much of it is constantly being lost from pores (stomata) on the underside of the leaves. Some plants have critical periods when a regular supply of water is important for a key stage of their development. Peas, beans, tomatoes, and other vegetables where the fruit is eaten have three critical periods for water requirements: when they are establishing, when they flower (to aid pollination and fruit set), and after the fruit has started to show obvious signs of swelling.

WHEN AND HOW OFTEN TO WATER Choosing the correct time of day to water can make huge savings in the amount of water lost to evaporation from the soil's surface. The soil is cool and the atmosphere is relatively moist in the early morning and late evening, and watering then will allow the water maximum time to soak in and be of use to the plants. Unfortunately, watering in the late evening can encourage slugs because it creates ideal conditions for their nocturnal feeding.

Watering frequency is a difficult factor to assess; every soil is different. Water moves down through the soil in a "moisture front." When it is applied, the top layer of soil becomes completely wet before the water reaches the next layer. Add enough water to thoroughly soak the soil to a reasonable depth, in order to encourage the root system to follow the water downward. Dig a hole and check the color of the soil to see how far the water has penetrated.

WATER REQUIREMENTS FOR SOME PLANTS (PER WEEK)	
Plant	Gallons/square yard
Clematis	1.8
Fruit bush	2.4
Plants in a hanging basket	1.3–2.6
Ornamental tree (five years old)	2.9
Bedding plants (established)	1.8–2.7
Lawn	4.6
Vegetables	4

ABOVE Some plants prefer a hot, dry situation with plenty of sunshine, and successful garden plants are the ones that can adapt to a wide range of growing conditions.

RIGHT Many fruits will produce one larger, earlier fruit at the tip of each cluster before the others around it have started to ripen. Picking these crown (or king) fruits will speed up the ripening of the rest.

AVOIDING DROUGHT In cases of dry weather, the amount of water lost from the leaves can exceed that taken in by the roots, causing the plant to wilt during the day and then slowly recover in the cooler evenings. However, a prolonged shortage of water can have long-term effects. These effects include the shedding of partially formed flower buds and flowers, poor color or a reduced size in the flowers that do open, premature leaf loss or early autumn color, fewer and smaller fruits that may be shed before they mature, and an increased susceptibility to pest and disease attack.

Young plants and those with soft, sappy growth are the most susceptible to drought, because their root systems are not sufficiently established to support the plant. Bedding plants and newly transplanted vegetable seedlings wilt rapidly in dry weather conditions.

Other plants and situations that create great risk in dry weather include: newly germinated seedlings; recently transplanted trees and shrubs (especially those transplanted as bare-root specimens, rather than container-grown plants); plants growing close to large and well-established competition, such as established trees and shrubs; and plants, such as climbers, growing close to walls that have foundations that absorb moisture or next to buildings that create a "rain-shadow," preventing much of the rainfall from reaching the soil.

Deep-rooted plants or those with thick, swollen roots are far better equipped to cope with dry conditions, but only after they are established, and their new roots have therefore penetrated the surrounding soil.

A brief drought period can be remedied by a thorough soaking, preferably allowing water to run gently onto the soil and soak in, rather than a quick splash with a garden hose. Long-term drought is much more difficult to rectify though, and the focus should be on measures to keep it from happening again.

Preparing the soil deeply with organic matter helps prevent drought by providing a reservoir of moisture for the roots. Adding well-rotted organic matter can increase the water-holding capacity in the top 6 in. of soil by 25 percent in the first year and as much as 60 percent if it is added again in the second year. Mulching the soil surface will reduce moisture lost from the top layers of the soil through evaporation, but where organic mulches are used, a layer of at least 2 in. is required to be effective.

Feeding

Few plants can sustain continued rapid growth without an injection of extra nutrients during the growing season because the development of both growth and flowers causes a huge drain on a plant's reserves. This is made even worse when plants are deadheaded and the spent flowerheads are removed, or when vegetables are harvested—these plant parts are an essential source of organic matter and nutrients that are lost to the plant if they are cut off. Unless some replacement nourishment is provided, the plant's overall performance will decline gradually.

However, rather than immediately reaching for a handful of fertilizer, it is important to consider what the plant actually needs, what result is intended, and how quickly the fertilizer will work. Certain plants require a specific

fertilizer, and without it, their growth may suffer. For plants that are intended to produce flowers and seeds, or plants that need to have their soft growth toughened for the onset of winter, a fertilizer low in nitrogen but high in phosphorus and potassium is ideal. On the other hand, if soft, leafy growth is desired for vegetables like cabbages, or if green, lush growth is required for a lawn, a fertilizer high in nitrogen but with lower quantities of potassium and phosphorus will help to produce the desired result.

Regardless of which type of fertilizer is being applied and whatever the aims and objectives of feeding the plants may be, there are a certain number of basic rules to follow. For fertilizers that have been bought, it is important to always follow the manufacturer's directions written on the container. Never feed plants that are wilting or growing in dry soil or compost without watering them sufficiently beforehand. Any fertilizer that is spilled directly onto any part of the plant should be washed off immediately to prevent scorching (especially in bright sunlight), unless you are using a foliar food. Only feed plants when they are actively growing, so that they gain the full benefit of the fertilizer.

ABOVE *Flowers intended for decorative use should be well watered the day before cutting to help them cope better after harvesting.*

BELOW *Avid flower arrangers appreciate a cutting border since its blossoms, fruits, and foliage are available throughout the seasons.*

Protecting cropping

Throughout the growing season, gardeners will regularly consider whether or not to provide some protection for their plants. There are many reasons why plants need some form of protection, depending on the time of year and the stage of the plants' development. In spring, plants need protection for a range of purposes, such as promoting earlier growth, cropping, or flowering. Early growth will also need to be protected from frost and cold winds. Advancing the growth of plants usually involves providing a warmer or more sheltered environment, so that plants can grow to a much larger size and be exposed to outdoor conditions when the weather is suitable.

EARLY PROTECTION   Greenhouses, cold frames, cloches, and plastic row covers are excellent structures for providing early protection to many plants. Even the hardiest plants can be frost-tender in the seedling stage.

Cloches made from glass, rigid plastic, Plexiglas, and plastic sheeting offer effective protection for low-growing plants and are ideal for short-term protection and giving plants an early start, especially vegetables and soft fruit, such as strawberries. However, in such protective structures the air around the plants can get very hot during the day, only to become very cool during the night and early hours of the morning. This fluctuation in temperatures may affect a few plants.

Unfortunately, protective structures can also be harmful for young plants that are easily damaged by sun scorch. Some additional screening may be necessary and should be applied on top of the structure as a precaution anyway. For small greenhouses, shade netting or blinds can be draped over the roof to filter the sun's rays. Alternatively, paint or spray the glass with a greenhouse shading paint.

BELOW LEFT   *Plants growing under cover will have the benefit of a warmer microclimate, and they will be ready to harvest slightly earlier than unprotected crops. Covering can also be used to provide a barrier against pests such as carrot rust flies.*

BELOW MIDDLE   *Gardeners like to experiment by growing new varieties in their greenhouses each year. Yellow-fruited tomatoes are a popular "novelty" plant, and have a sweeter flavor than their red-fruited counterparts.*

BELOW RIGHT   *Salad crops are a favorite summer meal, particularly for birds like wood pigeons. A protective covering of netting should thwart their plans for a dawn feast at the gardener's expense.*

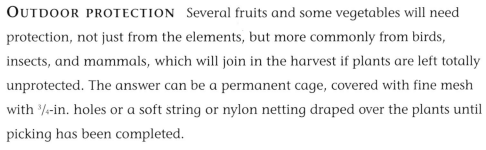

ABOVE *Any slight injury or damage to fruit, such as these bird peckings, will most certainly result in fungal spores entering the wound and causing the fruit to rot—possibly leading to the surrounding fruits becoming exposed and infected as well.*

LEFT *It is important to protect fruits early, as soon as they actually start to ripen. Once the birds begin to feed on a particular plant, they will often strip it bare before moving on to the next.*

OUTDOOR PROTECTION Several fruits and some vegetables will need protection, not just from the elements, but more commonly from birds, insects, and mammals, which will join in the harvest if plants are left totally unprotected. The answer can be a permanent cage, covered with fine mesh with ³/₄-in. holes or a soft string or nylon netting draped over the plants until picking has been completed.

Vegetables may face a few problems from unwanted visitors. Carrots are best protected by a covering of horticultural fleece, or garden fabric, to keep out rust flies. Young members of the brassica family, especially cauliflower, can be reduced to stalks overnight by marauding wood pigeons. Nets will be needed in order to prevent this particular pest, because they fly in and land close by before walking into the crop and feeding on it, which makes erecting strings a complete waste of time.

Fruits may also need additional help in the eventuality that the burden of fruit becomes so great that the plant may be physically damaged by the weight of it. The easiest way to prevent this is to select a strong stake that is at least 2 ft. taller than the tree and tie it, in an upright position, to the main stem of the tree. Run string lines from the top of the stake out to the branches, to provide support until the fruit is harvested. The string should be tied about two-thirds of the way along the branch to provide adequate support and protect the branch from snapping.

FRUITS THAT MAY NEED NETTING

Blackberries

Black currants

Blueberries

Cherries

Gooseberries

Grapes

Loganberries

Nectarines

Peaches

Raspberries

Red currants

Strawberries

White currants

PLANTS THAT ATTRACT PARTICULAR PESTS	
Plant	**Pest**
Basil	Aphids
Broad beans	Red spider mite
Chinese cabbage	Cornworms
Mustard	Wireworms
Nicotiana	Whiteflies

BELOW *There is no rule to say that flowers, fruits, and vegetables cannot be grown close together in the same border. In this particular case, the runner beans will harness nitrogen that the surrounding plants can use later.*

OPPOSITE PAGE *Nasturtiums are a popular companion plant for planting close to apples. Their proximity often helps deter woolly aphids from colonizing the apple trees.*

Companion planting

Many years ago, gardeners began to realize that certain plants will grow together and compliment each other, to the extent that they appear to grow less successfully when they are growing apart. Others seem to be more successful growing on their own—in fact, other plants seem to have difficulty growing close by.

Scientists have been able to establish that a number of plants actually produce chemicals that seep from their roots, fallen leaves or twigs that have an allelopathic effect on the surrounding soil. This acts to reduce competition from neighboring plants and helps to ward off pests and diseases, or reduce the harm they can do to certain plants. *Tagetes minima*, for instance, produces a root exudate that acts as a barrier to prevent the encroachment from perennial weeds such as bindweed and ground elder, as well as deterring eelworms.

Some companion plants can be used as attractants rather than repellents. Such plants may be used as "trap plants," to act as bait and draw a particular pest away from a crop onto a plant that it will live on quite happily. In effect, these trap plants will be totally sacrificed for the good of

the main crop. When a high population of a pest has congregated on the trap plant, the plant can be removed and burned, along with the pests.

Numerous advocates of companion planting know that certain plant combinations are beneficial because they reduce the need to use synthetically manufactured chemicals to combat some pests and diseases. However, what is not fully recorded yet is the ideal ratio of cropping plants to companion plants. If there are too few companion plants present, only a small proportion of the crop will actually receive protection, but if too many are present, crop yield may fall due to the competition between the cropping plants and their companions.

It is also worth remembering that companion planting can disrupt crop rotations, and may actually harbor some pests and diseases, enabling them to survive from one crop to the next.

SOME USEFUL COMPANION PLANT COMBINATIONS

Crop	Companion plant
Apple	Nasturtium
Asparagus	Basil, parsley, tomato
Bean, broad	Brassica, carrot, celeriac, celery, cucumber, potato, zucchini, most herbs
Bean, string	Celery, cucumber, potato, squash, strawberry, sweet corn, zucchini
Beet	Bean, brassica, garlic, kohlrabi, onion
Brassica	Beet, celeriac, celery, chard, dill, garlic, nasturtium, onion, pea, potato
Carrot	Chive, garlic, leek, lettuce, onion, pea, tomato
Celery and celeriac	Brassica, bean, leek, tomato
Chard	Bean, brassica, garlic, kohlrabi, onion
Cucumber, squash, zucchini	Bean, nasturtium, pea, radish, sweet corn
Eggplant	Bean
Leek	Carrot, celeriac, celery, garlic, onion
Lettuce	Carrot, cucumber, radish, squash, zucchini
Onion and Garlic	Beet, chard, lettuce, strawberry, summer savory
Pea	Bean, carrot, cucumber, radish, squash, sweet corn, turnip, zucchini
Potato	Bean, brassica, pea, sweet corn
Radish	Chervil, cucumber, lettuce, squash, zucchini
Rutabaga	Pea
Strawberry	Bean, lettuce, spinach
Sweet corn	Bean, cucumber, pea, potato, squash, zucchini
Tomato	Asparagus, basil, carrot, garlic, onion, parsley
Turnip	Pea

protection from bird attacks *All too often, the crop a gardener works so hard to produce is seen as a meal by the wildlife that are in the garden. It is worth remembering that most birds and mammals have a varied diet, and although they may be encouraged into the garden to feed on slugs and insects, they will still find ripening fruits and berries very tasty.*

Even if birds only nibble or peck at the odd fruit and leave it, this open wound will attract secondary feeders, such as wasps, or be open to fungal and bacterial infections that may then spread to surrounding fruits. Birds, in particular, rely heavily on their sense of smell (not color) to tell when fruit is ripening—which is why they often decimate the fruit of one plant before moving on to its neighbor. In this situation, protection is most essential, and it is important to protect the fruit before it actually starts to ripen, not after the birds have attacked it.

For large areas, various forms of mechanical bird repellents can be used, providing they are not too noisy. Make sure to use several different ones; the birds will become used to one type of device very quickly. For individual plants or small areas, a fine-mesh netting is the most effective method, but it must be suspended above the plants, rather than merely draped over them, so birds are unable to peck through.

AUTHOR'S TIP:
Netting

If the netting is allowed to sag, it may touch the plants (especially if it is windy). This can damage the plants and fruits and also allows birds to peck at the crop.

CLOCKWISE FROM TOP LEFT

Select sturdy stakes or bamboo canes, at least 3 ft. taller than the crop they are protecting, so they can be firmly anchored into the ground and still have a clearance of 1 ft. overhead. Insert the poles into the ground about 2 ft., with a distance of 6–10 ft. between them. Position them at least 1 ft. away from the plants.

Join some lateral supports to the upright supports using specially made brackets that interlock. Or, use old tennis balls with holes cut in them to grip the poles of the support structure.

When the structure is complete, drape the netting over it, starting with the roof and finishing with the sides and ends. Stretch the net tightly over the supports to prevent sagging.

Fix the bottom of the netting into the soil using wire pins. Rolling it around a stake helps to keep the net taut and makes pinning it into position much easier.

The netting can be attached to the supports using twist ties to hold the netting in place.

MATERIALS

Sturdy stakes or bamboo canes

Brackets that interlock (or old tennis balls with holes cut into them)

Fine-mesh netting

Wire pins

Twist ties or garden twine (optional)

plant CULTIVATION

Most cultivated plants, whether they originated in other countries and were introduced into our gardens or are selections or hybrids of our indigenous plants, are quite capable of growing no matter if they are cared for or left to grow wild. The major difference is that by cultivating plants, the gardener can "tame" them, that is, encourage them to grow in a particular fashion or to produce a desired result.

If the plants are ornamentals, they will be grown to provide decoration of some kind, either as individuals or as part of a design plan. With cropping plants, often the sole purpose of growing them is to harvest all or part of the plant, either as food or for some other use. They may even be required to act as a "trap" plant, to attract pests and diseases away from other plants, or as a pollinator for other edible plants.

The main reason plants tend to perform better, look healthier, grow bigger, and live longer when they are cultivated is that they do not have to fend for themselves, because the gardener is watching out for them. True cultivation of plants often involves taking away at least some of the plant's responsibility for caring for itself. With house plants and greenhouse plants, a large proportion of the plants' immediate climatic needs are provided by the sheltered environment in which they are growing.

Cultivating plants is not just a matter of providing conditions as close to the plant's native environment as possible, but it also involves providing better than natural conditions, to help the plant perform as required. In many respects the real skill of cultivating plants comes with the challenge of growing a range of unrelated plants close together in the same environment (even though these plants originate from all around the world) in an environment that may not be ideal for any of them. The range of plants available is always increasing and so is the gardener's desire to grow them.

RIGHT *Insects are always ready to visit flowers for nectar and pollen, regardless of whether or not the plants they feed on are native or exotic.*

cultivation

The cultivation of plants can be divided into two separate levels: first, keeping the plants alive and meeting their cultural needs, and second, experimenting to try to enhance the growth and performance of the plant. In truth, cultivation becomes a compromise between what is best for the plant and what is easier or more convenient for the gardener.

Plants do not grow in rows in the wild, but they do have to compete with a wide variety of neighboring plants, and very few gardens have the space to allow that to happen. In cultivation, growing plants in rows saves valuable space and makes managing them easier, although the competition between plants being grown close together tends to increase both their fertilizer and water requirements.

The close proximity and high population of one type of plant in a relatively small area also leads to a higher-than-average incidence of pest and disease problems, simply because they are drawn by the concentration of host plants.

The first aspect of cultivation is the most important, because keeping plants alive is the starting point for making any progress in development later on. Even experienced gardeners still have to go back to basics every time they start to grow a plant they have never grown before.

BELOW *When growing cropping plants, such as vegetables, it is important to allow them adequate space to grow and develop before they are ready for harvesting.*

Depending on where and how they are growing, many plants will be dependent on the gardener for most of the food and water they get. Plants growing in the garden should receive top dressings of fertilizer and organic matter, as well as water during dry periods, but there will also be periods when their roots will have to forage through the soil to get what they need.

The situation is very different for container-grown plants. The restrictions on their root area and the fact that they are isolated from the garden soil means that these plants rely entirely on what the gardener supplies them.

The second aspect of cultivation involves making an attempt to grow plants in a different way or in a different environment. This can be based partly on knowing how the plant has performed in the past and partly on trial and error to discover its adaptability and tolerances.

You may try to grow indoor plants out in the garden, for at least part of the year; try growing plants in peat-free compost for the first time or decide not to use any pesticides on edible crops. Even though the plants may be the same ones that you have grown for several years, changing the cultural regimen will influence their performance considerably. For instance, tomato plants will have different feeding and watering requirements depending on whether they are growing in a soil-based compost, a peat-based compost, or a peat-free compost.

Launching into a total change of regimen for the wrong reasons, like following a current fashion, is a mistake. The wise gardener knows that modifying how plants are grown in an attempt to improve a plant or crop means monitoring its progress and assessing which aspects of the change are actually improvements. It is a more sensible approach to change one cultural aspect at a time, until the new method is proved to be satisfactory.

Pinching

Growing plants, whether it is to produce flowers or a crop to eat, involves advance planning, especially when using plants that will be in the garden for more than one year. Part of this planning will be finding ways to encourage the plants to become what is expected of them.

Pinching, the removal of the soft growing tip using a finger and thumb, can be used to shape plants. Removing the tips of the shoots encourages young plants to produce lots of new side shoots and become much bushier in pattern. This is no different from the principle of clipping a topiary plant, only pinching is done by hand (not using shears or clippers).

Even annual plants can be trained in different ways to produce what the gardener sees as a more beneficial effect. Plants like sweet peas can be made to produce larger flowers by pinching off their support tendrils as they develop. This does mean that the plant has to be tied to its support, but the vast amount of energy the plant normally expends in supporting itself is channeled into the size and number of flowers produced.

Debudding

This practice is usually associated with flowers, but the removal of any buds, whether they are able to produce flowers or shoot growth, is still debudding.

ABOVE TOP *Geraniums can be made to grow in a more bushy pattern by pinching off the shoot tips, to stimulate side shoots to develop.*

ABOVE BOTTOM *Removing the leaf tendrils from sweet peas will direct more of the plant's energy into producing large flowers.*

RIGHT *Plants that are overcrowded and allowed to get scrambled up will look very attractive from a distance, but the quality of the individual flowers may actually be poor.*

For many years, competitive gardeners growing plants for exhibition have used the practice of debudding to manipulate the type and size of flowers their plants produce. To produce larger blooms than normal—and possibly slightly earlier in the season—they remove the lower (secondary) flower buds, from roses and chrysanthemums in particular. This pushes all of a plant's vigor into the remaining crown, or terminal, bud in the tip of its most dominant stem.

Working on a similar principle, removing growth buds from the stems of plants to leave the growing tip on its own is the system used to create plants, such as the standard fuchsia, on a tall, clean stem. Conversely, by removing the crown bud in the very top of the stem, it is possible to promote the growth of all of the lower flowers to develop at roughly the same time, and this is how spray chrysanthemums and spray carnations are produced.

Thinning

While some plants are hard to grow, others grow too well for their own good, making thinning a necessary task to reduce the competition either between individual plants or between shoots and branches on the same plant.

The most frequent use of thinning is among seedlings, where extra seed is sown to compensate for losses. If the ensuing germination is good, the competition can be so fierce that all the seedlings will suffer. By removing a portion of them to thin out the overall seedling population, the remaining plants then have room to develop and mature.

With some of the more rapidly maturing vegetables, such as carrots, radishes, and onions, the seedlings can be left for a slightly longer period before they are thinned so that the thinnings are large enough to harvest and eat, rather than just being thrown away.

When pruning overcrowded plants, the shoots can be thinned out by removing a portion, allowing those remaining to develop and mature.

ABOVE *Growing plants closer together will usually make them grow taller because they ultimately have to compete against one another for more sunlight.*

LEFT *Sunflowers will naturally grow tall, especially if they are given plenty of support. Their flowerheads follow the sun as it passes through the sky during the day.*

Weeds and weed control

Although most gardeners tend to refer to native indigenous plants as weeds, the true definition of a weed is any plant growing in a place where it is not wanted. The main reason indigenous plants can be such a problem is that they grow in their natural environment and are perfectly adapted to cope with the growing conditions. They also often have a longer growing season than many plants introduced from other parts of the world.

Weeds compete directly with ornamental and crop plants for light, nutrients, and water, as well as playing host to pests and diseases that can spread onto the crops as the season progresses. For instance, groundsel can harbor rust, mildew, and greenfly; chickweed can harbor red spider mites and whiteflies; and nightshades can play host to viruses and eelworms. These problems can migrate onto both ornamental and cropping plants, as some viruses are capable of surviving in the soil for many years.

ANNUALS   These have a very short life cycle, ranging from one to several months. They produce vast quantities of seed, which remain alive in the soil for years. Some annuals are able to produce around 60,000 viable seeds per square yard per year, hence the old saying "one year's seeds make seven years' weeds." Most of these seeds are found in the top 2 in. of soil and usually germinate when exposed to light by cultivations.

Killing annuals with shallow hoeing is quite an effective method of weed control, since the stem is severed from the root system just below soil level, preventing the stem from forming new roots as well as stopping the existing roots from producing a new stem. Timing is important; it must be done before the weeds start producing seeds.

ABOVE   *Plantains can be a real problem in lawns because their low rosette growth pattern covers the soil, killing the grass nearby due to the lack of light.*

BELOW LEFT   *Docks have a thick, fleshy taproot and produce large amounts of seed that is easily spread over a wide area.*

BELOW MIDDLE   *Some spurges (euphorbia) have explosive seed dispersal mechanisms that enable them to spread seeds a long way.*

BELOW RIGHT   *Both clover and dandelions can be difficult to eradicate without using chemicals—any small piece that is broken off a plant will soon form another plant and establish very quickly.*

PERENNIAL WEEDS Perennials have a life cycle of more than two years, and some appear to live almost indefinitely, often spreading through the garden. Many can reproduce by seeds, but also by other means, such as small segments of underground stem that break off and form new plants. For instance, couch grass (*Elytrigia repens*) is reputed to be capable of producing a new plant from segments as small as .05 in. long. Dandelion (*Taraxacum officinale*) can produce live seeds without pollination taking place. Others will produce runners, rhizomes, or stolons, which are all types of stems, modified to spread rapidly over or through the soil.

Digging up perennials is a good way of dealing with such weeds, provided the entire plant is removed. This method is ideal for small areas or where only a few weeds are present. It also helps to eradicate weeds growing close to the garden plants without risking damage to these nearby plants.

Controlling weeds

Most weeds are actually native plants that have evolved and adapted to their environment and growing conditions. If these native plants are not controlled, they will quickly colonize the garden, smothering most ornamental plants and spoiling crops.

CULTIVATIONS The simplest way to deal with all weeds is to physically remove them, either by pulling or digging them out of the soil or, if they are small, hoeing them off at soil level. The major problem with cultivations is that most weed seeds will start to germinate once exposed to daylight. Disturbing the soil and allowing more air into the surface layers creates an ideal seedbed, starting the weed "problem" all over again, and forcing the gardener into a cycle of regular cultivations.

MULCHING Probably derived from the German word "molsch," meaning "soft" or "starting to decay," mulching is the practice of covering the soil around the plants with a layer of additional material to block out light and help trap moisture. Inorganic, black plastic materials are often used as a mulch, because they help to warm up the soil in the spring by absorbing the sun's heat. Mulches are a most efficient weed barrier; with no air and little water available, many weeds will suffocate and die. Mulches are quite unattractive, but can be hidden beneath a thin layer of other material.

To block out sunlight fully, organic mulches must be applied as a layer at least 4 in. deep. By doing this, they will also improve the fertility of the soil below. Both organic and inorganic mulches are less useful against established perennial weeds, unless an entire area is sealed until the weeds die out, and planting is carried out through the mulch while it is in place.

ABOVE *Growing plants in rows makes it convenient to control weeds by cultural methods such as hoeing or raking.*

BELOW LEFT AND RIGHT *Man-made mulches, such as black plastic, may not be attractive to look at, but they are a very effective method of suppressing weeds.*

CHEMICAL WEED CONTROL   Any chemical that is used to kill weeds is called an "herbicide." They are preferred by some gardeners as an alternative to cultural weed control, and are the most effective method of controlling established perennial weeds. These chemicals are grouped according to their method of action:

• Contact chemicals: These are chemicals that only injure and kill the parts of the plant they come into contact with. This type of weed killer is most effective when used to control annual weeds.

• Residual chemicals: These are "soil acting" chemicals that are applied to the soil, and often persist in the soil for some months. They are taken up by the roots of the weeds, killing them slowly.

• Systemic chemicals: These chemicals are applied to the leaves of the weeds. They are absorbed and transported through the weed before killing it. These are the most effective means of controlling established perennial weeds.

PLANTING FOR WEED CONTROL   Planting vegetables close together will keep any sunlight from reaching the soil and can stop weed seeds from germinating. Some ornamental plants are useful to combat weeds, but they must have specific characteristics, including a low, spreading growth pattern with evergreen or coniferous growth to keep the soil covered in the spring, which is when most weed seeds germinate. Ground-cover planting is only effective if the soil is weed-free before planting begins.

ABOVE LEFT AND RIGHT *Waste products, such as grass clippings, can make an excellent mulch, but they must be well-composted or the heat they generate when fresh can harm the surrounding plants.*

BELOW *Inorganic material, such as gravel, slate, or stones, is an attractive way to control weeds, but is far less beneficial to the soil's fertility than organic mulches are.*

weed control

The simplest way to deal with weeds is to physically remove them, either by pulling them out by hand, digging them out of the soil, or, if they are small, hoeing them off at soil level. With hoeing, it is important to sever the weed seedlings at a point just between the root and the stem, as this causes both the root and the stem to die, giving less chance of regrowth.

Unfortunately, disturbing the soil surface and allowing more light and air into the upper layers creates an ideal seedbed, and so, although the existing weed seedlings are destroyed, the weed problem will start all over again.

For gardeners planting permanent beds of ornamental plants, various techniques can be used in order to control weeds (see pp.140–1). One successful method of keeping weeds at bay is to cultivate the soil (removing any obvious weeds) and then cover the whole area with a sheet of black or white plastic that is sealed around the edges. Any remaining weeds will try to grow under the plastic but will gradually be killed by the combination of a lack of light and an insufficiency of carbon dioxide. These particularly harsh growing conditions will force even perennial weeds to live off their reserves, and they, too, will eventually die of exhaustion. The plastic cover can be hidden with a covering of an organic mulch, such as shredded bark, or an inert material, such as gravel, in order to create a more attractive, finished look.

AUTHOR'S TIP:
How to know where to plant

It may seem odd to dig the holes first and then cover the bed with plastic, but the cold air from the holes will cause condensation to form on the plastic directly above it, which indicates where to cut the Xs for planting.

CLOCKWISE FROM TOP LEFT

Start by marking where each plant is going to be positioned, and dig a planting hole that is large enough to accommodate the whole root system.

Place a sheet of heavy-gauge black plastic over the bed and bury the edges at least 6 in. deep, stretching the plastic as tight as possible.

Cut an X in the plastic at the location where each plant is to be placed, and fold back the flaps of plastic to reveal the planting hole beneath.

Holding each plant, in turn, by its stem or leaves, gently remove it from its container. Holding the plant by its rootball, place it through the plastic into the hole positioning the base of the rootball at the bottom of the hole.

Using your hands or a trowel, pull the soil back into the hole around the plant, and tamp gently into place. Make sure the surface of the compost is covered with soil, and leave a slight depression around the stem. Immediately after planting, fold the plastic flaps back into position around the base of the plant.

Hide the plastic by covering it with a layer of gravel, spreading gravel evenly over the plastic.

TOOLS FOR THE JOB

1 spade

1 knife (to cut the Xs)

1 trowel (optional)

1 rake

MATERIALS

1 sheet of heavy-gauge black plastic

Plants

Compost

Gravel

Pollination

In some respects, the act of pollination can be a real dilemma for the gardener. The reason most plants go through a flowering process is to produce and receive pollen in order for fertilization to take place, which leads to the production of seeds.

DISADVANTAGES In the case of ornamental plants, it would suit the gardener if pollination did not take place unless the intention was to breed more plants. This is because once the flowers have been fertilized, they will start to develop seeds, and as these seeds develop, there is a natural tendency for the plant to stop producing more flowers. So, if you want the plant to continue flowering, it is essential to deadhead to keep seeds from forming.

ADVANTAGES For various edible plants, extra measures have to be taken to ensure that the best possible pollination can occur so the plant is fertilized and produces as much fruit or seed as possible.

For fruit—tree fruit in particular—it is important to make sure that closely related cultivars are planted near one another so cross-pollination can take place (which is often essential for fertilization to occur). In these cases, the plants are not only selected to be compatible with one another, but their flowering periods must also coincide as closely as possible.

ENCOURAGING POLLINATION Where plants are positioned and how they are arranged in relation to one another can have a strong bearing on how well they are pollinated. Where plants are pollinated by wind, or some other form of air turbulence, they stand a better chance of pollinating both

ABOVE *Some flowers have markings on the petals that act as guides to lead visiting pollinating insects to the areas of the flower where the nectar can be found.*

BELOW LEFT *It is easy to consider insects garden pests, but the majority are beneficial. They act as predators to damaging insects and, more important, are the main agents of pollination for the plants we grow.*

BELOW RIGHT *The long mouthparts of butterflies and moths are very important for the pollination of plants with long, narrow, tubular flowers.*

themselves and their near neighbors if they are planted close together in rows (or, in the case of sweet corn, in blocks). However, the strength of the wind on exposed, windy sites will often reduce pollination.

The same is true for insect-pollinated plants: If the site is exposed, the insects will not fly in strong winds. To get around this problem, some plants, such as scarlet runners and tomatoes, can be tapped or sprayed with water to shake pollen loose and therefore improve pollination, or the pollen can be transferred by hand with a small, soft brush.

Plants that must be cross-pollinated will need more than one cultivar present so that they are able to pollinate one another. Where possible, these plants should be arranged in rows, with the plants almost touching. This is because many pollinating insects (bees in particular) tend to work along a row, rather than flitting across rows or from plant to plant. Also, numerous pollinating insects prefer to keep foraging on a particular type of pollen for several days, so the most difficult task for the gardener is to get them interested in his crop in the first place.

In the modern garden, where both organic and inorganic chemicals are so commonly used, it is important to try to avoid using sprays while the plants are in flower. Even if the chemicals used are not harmful to pollinating insects, the "taint," or smell, of a chemical can be enough to deter these beneficial insects at a time when gardeners and their plants need them the most.

ABOVE *There can be some fierce competition between plants to attract pollinating insects. Some plants have actually evolved to prevent self-pollination or attract only certain insects.*

BELOW *Many plants produce flowers that can only be pollinated over a short period. This makes the use of perfume and color crucial in order to attract insects.*

building a cloche

This cloche, or row cover, can be easily constructed on any sheltered area with well-drained soil that is reasonably fertile and free from perennial weeds. It is ideal for giving plants an early start in spring—up to three weeks ahead of unprotected plants—which can be important for early vegetables and such low-growing fruits as strawberries.

This type of structure is ideal for offering protection from spring frosts, and where certain types of horticultural fleece are used, it can also offer some protection from pests like carrot rust flies. Alternatively, when the plants begin to crop, the covering can be replaced with different grades of netting, in order to prevent the produce from being harvested by marauding birds and mammals.

If the cloche is built correctly, it should be quite easy to lift up the plastic on either side and tie it loosely at the top to gain access to the beds in order to harvest crops or for general maintenance. On windy sites, it is best to position the cloche so that one end faces into the wind. This will offer a smaller surface area to the wind, and it is much easier to reinforce than the sides along the length of the row cover.

For this type of construction, the most expensive item will be the wire, but this will probably last for up to twenty years, while the plastic will last about two to three seasons.

AUTHOR'S TIP:
Using opaque plastic

For areas that become very hot and sunny during the summer months, it is best to use opaque rather than clear plastic; this will reduce the chances of plants' being scorched by the bright sunlight.

CLOCKWISE FROM TOP LEFT

To make the hoops, cut an 8-ft. length of heavy-gauge galvanized wire. Grip a section of broom handle between the jaws of the workbench with 4 in. rising above the bench top. Wrap the wire once around the handle to form a loop (eyelet), leaving a 1-ft. leg. Turn the wire over and repeat on the other end to produce a length of wire with two loops close to each end.

Prepare the cloche bed by laying two parallel guidelines 3 ft. apart in order to mark the edges of the beds and keep them straight. Once the beds have been cultivated, push the wire hoops in close to the guidelines, spaced about 3 ft. apart along the bed. Push the legs into the soil so that the eyelets are at soil level.

At each end of the bed, drive a length of wooden batten into the soil, level with the top of the end hoops, and nail the hoop to the batten.

When the hoops are in position, place the plastic cover over them carefully.

Stretch the plastic tightly over the hoops and tie it to the eyelets with plastic cord.

Secure the ends of the plastic by burying the ends in the soil about 1 ft. deep.

TOOLS FOR THE JOB

1 workbench

1 pair of pliers

2 guidelines

1 hammer

1 spade

MATERIALS

8-ft. length of heavy-gauge galvanized wire

Broom handle

2 wooden battens

Nails

Plastic cover

Plastic cord (nonrotting kind)

harvest
HOME

Harvesting, whether it is of flowers or a food crop, is the most rewarding aspect of gardening, and it is especially enjoyable when the produce collected is edible. This is the time of the year when the gardener reaps the reward of the season's labors. Freshly picked produce has more flavor than anything bought in a local grocery store or supermarket.

Fruits, vegetables, and herbs can all be used fresh and any surplus can often be stored for later use. However, harvesting has its problems, and it is important to be aware that produce does not actually improve in storage. In fact, make sure to always store only the best of what is available during harvesting. The work carried out earlier in the year can be easily wasted by not harvesting a crop until it has passed its peak.

Careful handling of the crop is essential to reduce damage, which can cause rapid deterioration and excessive waste. Plant selection is also helpful, since certain fruits and vegetables have better storage qualities than others. Many new cultivars are hybrids, bred for a specific purpose, such as the production of uniform plants with a predictable performance, and often have a short (but very specific) harvesting period. Several older cultivars have a longer harvesting period, and the crop is ready in smaller amounts, thus spreading out the harvest more evenly and avoiding a glut period.

Plant health also significantly affects how well the crop stores. Some nutrient deficiencies and pest and disease problems only become apparent during storage. Harvesting and storage cannot be viewed in isolation; they are an integral part of growing and producing a crop. At this point it is well worth remembering that plants that have been forced or advanced in some way will often be far more sensitive and vulnerable to poor handling or less than ideal storage conditions. Also, the yield is usually lower from these earlier crops when compared with natural season crops.

RIGHT *Fresh produce should be placed out of direct sunlight in a cool, dark place as soon as possible after harvesting. This will help to slow down the ripening process.*

picking and handling

For a large number of fruits and vegetables, it is quite difficult to assess just when the correct time for harvesting the produce is. If a gardener has any doubts at all about when to harvest, the golden rule is that it is far better to harvest slightly early, rather than too late. The produce will actually continue to live after picking, so will also continue to ripen. If you are storing the produce, make sure that it has not been damaged in any way.

ABOVE *When picking, be sure you select only fruits that are ripe enough and leave the rest to mature on the plant.*

BELOW *Fruit scattered over the ground can indicate an excessively heavy crop or an infestation of pests and disease, causing the fruit to abort.*

Picking

Unless you have been growing fruit for a while, it can be difficult to assess when to start picking. To help the inexperienced gardener, there are certain clues to watch for, such as the first true windfalls for instance—if the fallen fruits appear to be free from any infestation (that might otherwise have contributed to their fall), then they may well be ripe. Also, test the adhesion of the fruit by lifting it in the palm of your hand and turning it carefully. The fruit is ready for picking if it comes away from the tree easily with its stalk intact. Some fruit crops will produce ripe fruit in sequence, starting with the main, or "tip," fruit first, followed by those immediately behind the tip.

Early apple cultivars should be picked before they are fully ripe and before their texture becomes soft and mealy (the seeds are often not fully brown when the fruits are picked). Be sure to pick the ripest, best-colored fruits first, which are usually located near the top of the tree and on the sunniest side. There is not much point in storing the early maturing cultivars such as 'Discovery,' 'James Grieve,' and 'Worcester Pearmain,' because they have quite a limited storage life and do not keep well. For these particular cultivars, the best approach is to watch them very closely in order to see which ones are ready for picking and harvest them directly from the tree for immediate use.

For most cultivars of apple, the best test to see how ripe they are is simply to select one and cut it open across the middle to observe the color of the seeds. If they are turning a dark brown (seed color does vary depending on the cultivar), it is likely that they are ready for picking.

There are also some cultivars of pear that do not keep well, such as 'Clapp's Favourite' and 'Jargonelle.' Harvest these as soon as they are ready and use them immediately. All other cultivars should be harvested before they reach maturity. Cultivars like 'Beth,' 'Williams Bon Chrétien,' and 'Gorham' all ripen very quickly after picking and should therefore be used as quickly as possible.

Handling

All fruit should be handled as little as possible, and as gently as possible. For many fruits, and especially those that are going to be stored, the whole idea of harvesting is to check, or interrupt, the ripening process, so that the fruit does not enter its final phase, rotting down to release its seeds. Every ripening fruit respires, or "breathes," and the aim of storage is to slow down respiration. Any fruit that has been damaged will respire at a faster rate around the injured cells and cause the fruit to ripen more quickly. This will also affect its neighbors, which are influenced by the gases being released.

Start picking fruit in the morning, once the dew has dried from the fruits' surface, as the dampness may encourage rotting. Place the fruit somewhere cool after picking to lower its temperature. This will slow down ripening and is particularly important for bush fruits that can only be eaten fresh for a limited time. Do not cover the fruit for long periods; this will trap the heat and natural gases that are released when fruits ripen, and, in turn, will speed up the ripening process of the surrounding fruit.

Storage and preservation

It really does not matter which method of storage is chosen for which particular crop. If the produce is not in peak condition, it has already begun to deteriorate. In this situation, storage will be quite pointless.

DRY STORAGE Some fruits and vegetables can be stored in a cool, dark, frost-free place, such as a garage or shed. Apples and pears are best laid on trays and inspected regularly for rot. They will keep longer if wrapped in tissue paper. Apples can also be stored in plastic bags, which reduce shrivelling and keep the fruit clean. Thin plastic bags that hold about 5 lbs. of fruit should be used, with the mouth of the bag folded over but not sealed. Small holes should be made in different parts of the bag to allow air to circulate around the fruit. If the cooking apple 'Bramleys Seedling' is stored in this way, more holes should be made, as the fruit can be spoiled by a buildup of carbon dioxide, which causes brown blotches on the flesh. As with other methods of storage, they should be kept in a cool, dark, frost-free place and inspected regularly for rot.

Pears prefer lower storage temperatures than apples and will store well in the refrigerator, provided the temperature is kept above freezing. This is true of many soft fruits and salad vegetables too.

A number of herbs, vegetables, and even fruits, such as grapes, can be hung in sheds and garages, and, provided that the structure is dry and frost-free, they will keep for weeks. Herbs are usually hung in bunches, either open or enclosed in dry paper bags, while vegetables are strung up or hung in nets for good air circulation.

COOL, DAMP STORAGE Many root vegetables can be stored in moist sand and placed in a cool, dark place where they will keep quite well for several months. Although this method of storage is often seen purely as a method of overwintering, it can be used in the summer for roots such as beets, which will become very hard and woody from midsummer onward as they mature. This method of storage is a much better alternative to leaving the crop in the ground to spoil.

FREEZING FRUITS AND VEGETABLES For the gardener, home freezers brought a whole new dimension to storing surplus summer produce that might otherwise have gone to waste. The most important thing is to harvest, prepare, and store the produce while it is still in peak condition—storing inferior produce is a complete waste of time. Some crops freeze better than others, and even some individual cultivars will freeze better than others.

ABOVE *Wrapping individual fruits keeps them in good condition, protects the skins, and also reduces the spread of disease from one infected fruit to its surrounding neighbors.*

BELOW *Crops that store quantities of water can be ruined by winter frost damage, so some method of insulation is essential.*

VEGETABLES THAT CAN BE DRY STORED

Beans	Peas
Cabbage	Potatoes
Chilies	Squash
Garlic	Tomatoes
Onions	

FRUITS AND VEGETABLES SUITABLE FOR FREEZING

Frozen when dry

Apples

Blackberries

Blueberries

Cherries

Currants

Damsons

Figs

Gooseberries

Greengages

Loganberries

Mulberries

Raspberries

Rhubarb

Strawberries

Kale

Kohlrabi

Parsnips

Peas

Potatoes

Rutabaga

Spinach

Spring onions

Sprouting broccoli

Squash

String beans

Sweet corn

Tomatoes

Turnips

Zucchini

In sugar/syrup

Apricots

Grapes

Melons

Pears

Plums

Quince

Blanched

Asparagus

Beets

Broad beans

Broccoli

Brussels sprouts

Cabbage

Carrots

Cauliflower

Eggplant

Shredded, pureed, diced, or sliced

Cabbage

Cauliflower

Celery

Eggplant

Kohlrabi

Rutabaga

Squash

Turnips

Frozen when young

Beets

Carrots

Parsnips

Turnips

fruit directory

Even the smallest garden has room to grow fruit. The increasing number of slow-growing or dwarf plants means that fruit growing is becoming more accessible all of the time, whether it is in a pot or tucked into a corner of the garden.

FRUIT DESCRIPTIONS

TOP FRUIT	PLANT TYPES	USES	PROPAGATION	COMMENTS
	Apricot Woody perennial that needs a well-drained soil but must have shelter.	Large, round fruits highly flavored and popular for desserts.	By budding or grafting onto a rootstock of known vigor.	The cultivar 'Moorpark' is the most reliable performer of all.
	Apple Woody perennial tree that prefers a deep, fertile, well-drained soil.	Swollen, edible fruits eaten cooked or raw over a long season.	By budding or grafting onto a rootstock of known vigor.	Interplant with nasturtiums to deter woolly aphids.
	Cherry Woody, perennial tree that prefers a deep, fertile, well-drained soil.	Clusters of small edible fruits eaten cooked or fresh over a short season.	By budding or grafting onto a rootstock of known vigor.	'Stella' is the easiest cultivar to grow; it is self-fertilizing.
	Damson Woody perennial tree that prefers a deep, fertile, well-drained soil.	Round or plum-shaped edible fruits eaten cooked or raw.	By budding or grafting onto a rootstock of known vigor.	The cultivar 'Merryweather' is self-fertilizing and reliable.
	Grape A vigorous, climbing woody plant. Prefers sun and a deep, fertile soil.	Bunches of rounded fruits, black, red, or pale yellowish-green in color.	By cuttings or grafting onto a rootstock of known vigor.	The leaves are also edible.
	Greengage Woody perennial tree that prefers a deep, fertile, well-drained soil.	Round or plum-shaped edible fruits are eaten cooked or raw.	By budding or grafting onto a rootstock of known vigor.	'Cambridge Gage' is partially self-fertilizing and the easiest to grow.
	Kiwi Fruit A vigorous, climbing woody plant. Prefers sun and a deep, fertile soil.	Slice through the rough, hairy peel to find a fleshy, green inside that is eaten raw.	By cuttings or grafting onto a rootstock of known vigor.	The late-flowering cultivar 'Hayward' is the most reliable plant to grow.
	Kumquat Woody perennial that needs a well-drained soil and must have shelter.	Small, yellow fruits that may be eaten without being peeled.	By budding or grafting onto a rootstock of known vigor.	This is the hardiest member of the citrus fruits.
	Lemon Woody perennial that needs a well-drained soil and a sheltered site.	Oval to round-shaped fruits from which you squeeze the juice to use as part of a seasoning.	By budding or grafting onto a rootstock of known vigor.	In order to do well, these plants prefer to grow in a fairly constant temperature.
	Lime Woody perennial that needs a well-drained soil and a sheltered site.	Small, green, rounded fruits with a thin skin. Mostly used for its juice.	By budding or grafting onto a rootstock of known vigor.	There are varieties with sweet- or sour-tasting fruits available.
	Nectarine Woody perennial that needs a well-drained soil and must have shelter.	Large round fruits, highly flavored and popular for desserts.	By budding or grafting onto a rootstock of known vigor.	The cultivar 'Early Rivers' produces large crops and self-fertilizes.

FRUIT DESCRIPTIONS

TOP FRUIT	PLANT TYPES	USES	PROPAGATION	COMMENTS
	Peach Woody perennial that needs a well-drained soil and must have shelter.	Large, round fruits, highly flavored and popular for desserts.	By budding or grafting onto a rootstock of known vigor.	The cultivar 'Peregrine' is self-fertile.
	Pear Woody perennial tree that prefers a deep, fertile, well-drained soil.	Swollen edible fruits eaten cooked or raw over a long season.	By budding or grafting onto a rootstock of known vigor.	'Conference' is the most reliable performer.
	Plum Woody perennial tree that prefers a deep, fertile, well-drained soil.	Round, edible fruits are eaten cooked or raw.	By budding or grafting onto a rootstock of known vigor.	'Opal' is self-fertilizing and produces large crops.

SOFT FRUIT DESCRIPTIONS

	Black currant A woody perennial bush that prefers a deep, fertile, well-drained soil.	Clusters of small edible fruits eaten fresh or cooked and preserved.	Increased by hard-wood cuttings.	The cultivar 'Ben Sarek' is resistant to mildew and late frosts.
	Blueberry A woody perennial bush. Prefers moist, acid soil and an open, sunny site.	Clusters of small, rounded, black, edible fruits eaten either fresh or cooked.	By cuttings or simple layering to produce new plants.	'Bluecrop' produces the best yields and is ideal for a wet soil.
	Briar Fruit A woody perennial plant. Prefers a deep, fertile, well-drained soil.	Clusters of large to medium edible fruits eaten fresh or cooked.	By cuttings or tip layering to produce new plants.	Vigorous, rambling, heavy-cropping plants that need a lot of space.
	Mulberry Woody perennial tree that prefers a deep, fertile, well-drained soil.	Clusters of large to medium edible fruits eaten fresh or cooked.	By cuttings or simple layering to produce new plants.	The black mulberry is the best fruiting type.
	Gooseberry A woody perennial bush that prefers a deep, fertile, well-drained soil.	Groups of medium-sized edible fruits eaten either cooked or raw.	Increased by hard-wood cuttings.	The cultivar 'Greenfinch' is resistant to mildew and leafspot.
	Raspberry A woody perennial bush that prefers a deep, fertile, well-drained soil.	Groups of medium-sized edible fruits eaten either cooked or raw.	By division of woody clumps to produce new plants.	Grow 'Malling Jewel' for its compact habit and disease tolerance.
	Red currant A woody perennial bush that prefers full sun and a deep, fertile soil.	Clusters of small edible fruits eaten fresh or cooked and preserved.	Increased by hardwood cuttings.	The cultivar 'Junifer' is well reputed for its disease resistance.
	Rhubarb A long-lived herbaceous perennial. Prefers a moist, well-drained soil.	Edible leaf stalks are cooked and eaten as a fruit.	Propagated by division of the "crowns" to form new plants.	Rhubarb leaves in planting trenches may deter clubroot on brassicas.
	Strawberry Short-lived herbaceous perennial. Prefers deep, fertile, well-drained soil.	Groups of medium-sized edible fruits eaten either fresh or cooked.	Increased by runners or cuttings taken from an older plant.	Plant onions close to strawberries to increase disease resistance.

top (tree) fruits

Apples

A highly versatile fruit, providing a wide variety of flavors and uses, with a long cropping and storing season running from late summer to midspring. They grow well in most soils, but tend to prefer a deep, well-drained soil that will not dry out too quickly in the summer. Most trees need cross-pollinating with another cultivar in order to produce fruit. Tree and bush forms usually require moderate pruning in winter to stimulate growth or, alternatively, in summer to encourage next season's fruit, so that they crop well on a regular basis and maintain an open, well-balanced structure. ❀ ❀ ❀

Yield: 22–110 lbs. per plant.

Cherries

Sweet cherries are ideal for eating fresh on their own as a dessert, and they can also be cooked. They flower very early, so they need shelter and protection, and are quite vigorous so require plenty of room. They are often trained against a wall for these particular reasons. All pruning should be done in the summer in order to reduce shoot growth and promote fruit bud formation. Some cultivars are self-fertilizing and can be grown as single plants. Fruits should be harvested when they are slightly soft to the touch. Fruits that are to be frozen should be picked while still firm. ❀ ❀ ❀ ❀ ❀

Yield: 11–22 lbs. per plant.

Peaches

These fruits are much hardier than many gardeners realize, but they do need a warm, sunny, sheltered position in order to perform well. They are usually trained against a south-facing wall exposed to plenty of sun and, for this specific reason, are frequently grown as a fan-trained tree. They can also be grown as single plants, as almost all are self-fertilizing and do not require a pollinator. Spring pruning is necessary in order to provide a regular supply of new shoots to replace the old fruit-bearing branches, which ought to be removed immediately after fruit picking. The fruit is ripe for picking when the flesh yields to gentle pressure when squeezed. ❀ ❀ ❀ ❀ ❀

Yield: 20 lbs. per plant.

Pears

Pears can be eaten fresh, used in desserts, cooked, or preserved. They prefer a warmer climate than most apples, but are almost as easy to grow. They tend to flower earlier and thus are more susceptible to spring frost damage. They require a deep, fertile soil that is moisture-retentive, because they are quite sensitive to drought. Most forms require some moderate pruning in winter to stimulate next season's growth and fruit, and they are happy to be pruned hard. The fruits must be picked before they ripen or they will rot almost immediately in storage. ❀ ❀ ❀ ❀

Yield: 9–13 lbs. per plant.

Plums and greengages

Both these fruits can be eaten fresh or used for cooking, canning, or jam making. Greengages have a better flavor, though they tend to produce fewer fruits than plums. They both need a warm, sheltered site that will attract pollinating insects while also protecting them from the risk of frost damage. Several cultivars need to be grown close together in order to ensure that they receive adequate pollination. They prefer a deep, well-drained soil, and should be summer-pruned to thin out overcrowded branches and remove some completely. The fruits do not store well and should be eaten within a few days of harvest, which runs from midsummer to midautumn. ❀ ❀ ❀ ❀

Yield: 20–40 lbs. per plant.

ABOVE LEFT *By growing a range of different cultivars and storing them in ideal conditions, it is possible to have fresh, homegrown apples for about ten months of the year.*

ABOVE RIGHT *These small, round fruits are simply delicious but must be eaten or cooked immediately. Ripe cherries need protection from birds.*

CENTER LEFT *Plums come in a range of colors from almost black to a very pale greenish-yellow. Once the fruits are ripe, they must be eaten or cooked within a few days, before they deteriorate.*

CENTER RIGHT *Pears must be picked before they are ripe, since they are easily bruised when ripe and start to rot very quickly. Stored pears should be allowed to reach room temperature for a day before they are eaten.*

BOTTOM *Almost all cultivars of peach produce fruits with a pinkish-red skin, but the color of the flesh varies from yellow to white or pink.*

berries and soft fruits

Blackberries

These vigorous, trailing, prickly plants are capable of producing large crops of delicious, large, glossy blackberries. There are thornless cultivars, such as 'Oregon Thornless' and 'Smoothstem.' They usually prefer a sheltered, sunny position but can tolerate partial shade. For easier management, blackberries are grown in rows and trained along horizontal wires. Keep the plants well-watered in dry periods to help the fruits swell and to keep the new shoots growing rapidly. Prune the old fruiting canes to ground level immediately after cropping has ended. The fruit is ideal for dessert, pies, jam, freezing, or winemaking. ✿ ✿ ✿ ✿ ✿ ✿ ✿

Yield: 15 lbs. per plant.

Black currants

Black currants are possibly the easiest soft fruits to grow. They form vigorous bushes that need plenty of room in order to grow well. They prefer an open, sunny position, and a very fertile, well-drained but also moisture-retentive site. The plants need to be watered thoroughly in dry periods, especially when the fruit is swelling; the roots are shallow and can easily suffer from drought. Prune in the autumn immediately after leaf-fall, removing one quarter of the total number of stems, starting with the oldest. The berries ripen by midsummer, and are ideal for making drinks, pies, jams, and eating fresh in desserts. ✿ ✿ ✿ ✿ ✿

Yield: about 6–7 lbs. per bush.

Figs

These are among the oldest fruits in cultivation. They prefer a deep, fertile, slightly alkaline soil, and are often planted in a lined pit to restrict their size. In the spring, feed the trees with an organic mulch laid 4 in. deep to retain moisture, and keep them well-watered in dry summer periods to prevent premature fruit drop. Figs must be allowed to ripen on the tree, and can be picked when the flesh yields to gentle pressure when squeezed between finger and thumb. The fruit is ideal for eating fresh and can be preserved. ✿ ✿ ✿ ✿ ✿ ✿

Yield: 10 lbs per plant.

Gooseberries

Gooseberries tend to grow well in a sheltered, sunny position or partial shade. They require a well-drained but moisture-retentive, fertile soil. They are one of the earliest-flowering soft fruits and may therefore need extra protection from spring frosts. Prune in early spring because birds, such as finches, often feed on the buds in the winter and this damaged wood may need to be removed thoroughly. Fruits start their ripening process from midsummer onward, turning either yellow, creamy-white, or red depending on the cultivar, and gradually softening as they ripen. Gooseberries can be used for cooking, jam, wines, or desserts, and can also be frozen. ✿ ✿ ✿ ✿ ✿

Yield: about 2 lbs. per bush.

Grapes

Fruit color varies from dark purple to greenish-white and yellow depending on the cultivar. Grapes can be eaten fresh, processed for juice, or used in winemaking. Any moisture-retentive, well-drained soil, preferably with some added organic matter, is ideal. Pruning the plants involves cutting out all old, fruited wood to leave three replacement shoots. Two of the shoots should then be tied down, one on either side of the center and the third shoot pruned back to leave three strong buds. Cut ripe bunches with a short section of stalk, placing them in a container lined with tissue paper. ✿ ✿ ✿ ✿ ✿ ✿

Yield: 30 lbs. per plant.

TOP *While growing on the plant, blackberries are well protected by an array of needle-sharp spines on leaves and stems.*

CENTER LEFT *This strange, exotic-looking fruit is green, often with reddish markings, and has a "flask" shape. Figs can be dried, although they taste better eaten fresh from the tree.*

CENTER RIGHT *There are green-, yellow-, white-, and red-berried cultivars of gooseberry. Those used for cooking are harvested while green, those for dessert are allowed to change color before picking.*

FAR RIGHT *Whether the fruit is black or white in color, grapes are much easier to grow than many gardeners realize.*

BOTTOM *These delicious black currants are rich in vitamin C. Pick the fruits when their skins have turned black and have a shiny surface.*

berries and soft fruits ❀ 159

berries and soft fruits

Kiwi fruit

This is an extremely vigorous climbing plant that produces large, hairy-skinned, gooseberry-like fruit. Male and female flowers are actually carried on separate plants, and both must be planted in order for a crop of fruit to be produced. You should arrange them with one male plant next to eight or nine female plants. They grow well in a sheltered, sunny position but can also grow in partial shade. What they do need is a deep, well-drained, fertile soil. The fruits are fully ripe when they begin to feel soft to the touch if squeezed, and can be picked by snipping through the fruit stalk with a pruner. The cultivar that crops the most reliably is 'Hayward,' especially if the cultivar 'Tomuri' is used as the pollinator. ❋ ❋ ❋ ❋ ❋ ❋

Yield: 30 lbs. per plant.

Raspberries

These plants prefer cool seasons and plenty of moisture, in a well-drained, fertile soil that is very rich in organic matter and has a pH between 5.5 and 7. They prefer a sheltered, sunny position but benefit greatly from a mulch with organic matter to a depth of 4 in. Summer-fruiting types should be pruned immediately after the crop has been picked, and this will involve the complete removal of all canes that have just fruited. The fruit can be used for fresh desserts, cooking, and jam, as well as freezing. ❋ ❋ ❋

Yield: 9 oz. per plant.

Red currants

Red currants prefer an open, sunny position in order to grow well. Notably, white currants are a variety of red currant. Almost any soil will do, provided it is well-drained, with plenty of added bulky organic matter. Red currants are quite vigorous and must have a clear stem, or "leg," of at least 6–8 in. in order to prevent the fruit from trailing on the ground if the branches are too low. The fruit is used for desserts, jam, jelly, or winemaking. Red currants are rather high in pectin and therefore are often added to other fruits when being used for making jam. ❋ ❋ ❋ ❋ ❋ ❋

Yield: about 9 lbs. per plant.

Rhubarb

This herbaceous perennial is technically a vegetable and is grown for its edible leaf stalks, which can be used as the ingredients for several delicious desserts from midspring onward, making it one of the earliest fresh fruits available. The plants ("crowns") must be kept well-mulched, moist, and well-fed after harvesting. The crop is ready when the stalks are about 1 ft. long and deep pink in color. Harvest by gently pulling them from the crown with a twisting motion. Be sure to discard the leaves, as they are NOT edible. The crop can be forced by covering it with loose straw as a means of promoting early growth. ❋ ❋ ❋

Yield: 6 lbs. per plant.

Strawberries

Strawberries are relatively short-lived, fruiting, herbaceous plants that only have a cropping life of approximately three years, and will grow in most well-drained soils. Summer-fruiting strawberries produce most of their fruit over a one-month period, but the cropping season can be extended by carefully selecting the cultivars grown. Cut off any runners bearing new young plants in the summer, and cut the foliage down to about 4 in. above ground level in the autumn after the fruit has been picked. Pick the fruit every other day, complete with stalks, when they are red over three-quarters of their total surface. ❋ ❋ ❋ ❋ ❋

Yield: 1 lb. per plant.

TOP *Red currants are picked by gathering the whole bunch, or "strig," by the stalk to avoid damaging the berries when harvesting.*

CENTER LEFT *The rough, hairy coat on the outside of a kiwi fruit gives little indication of the succulent contents inside. This fruit is now a popular choice for breakfast.*

CENTER RIGHT *Really a vegetable, rhubarb is grown for its pinkish-red leaf stalks, which can be "forced" to make them the earliest homegrown outdoor "fruit."*

FAR LEFT *Raspberries grow in clusters of conical-shaped berries. Some cultivars are grown entirely for eating fresh because of their rich, delicious flavor.*

BOTTOM *This is the soft fruit most often associated with summer. A crop of strawberries should be harvested when the berries have turned almost completely red.*

picking and storing soft fruit

One of the great delights of summer gardening is the selection of fruits, particularly berries and soft fruits, to be harvested and eaten or stored. They provide a range of flavors that is difficult to beat, but only if they are grown well and harvested with care. All soft fruit must be picked carefully, as any damage makes the appearance of the fruit unsightly, severely limits its storage qualities, and increases the risk of fungal mold infection.

Ideally, the fruit should be in a dry condition when picked, with no moisture on the surface. Wetness and overripeness cause the fruit to deteriorate very rapidly when handled. The ideal stage for picking is when the fruits are firm and fully colored, but not fully ripe; they should part easily from the plant. Separate blackberries, loganberries, and raspberries from the plant with a gentle pull, leaving the core, or plug, behind. Gooseberries and strawberries are picked by breaking the stalk, and currants are often taken off as bunches, or "strigs," complete with their stalks.

Provided it is done with care, it is possible to allow some fruits to gather in the palm of your hand before they are transferred to a picking container. Soft fruits do not store well for long periods of time unless they are frozen or preserved, and they are best eaten within 24 hours of being harvested. However, fruits harvested for jam or jelly need not be handled quite so carefully, as long as they are cooked within a few hours of picking.

AUTHOR'S TIP:
Preventing mold

When storing soft fruits, be sure that they are left in a cool, dark place, and, most important, do NOT wash the fruit to cool it, since this will encourage mold and spoil the fruit.

CLOCKWISE FROM TOP LEFT

A week before picking, check the stage of development of the fruit. Some plants may need a light trim to increase fruit visibility, reduce humidity around the fruit, and allow more sunlight into it.

Wash the containers to reduce the amount of dirt and fungal spores. This is most important if they have been used before.

Start picking on the sunniest side of the plant, where the surface of each fruit is driest. Gently pull the fruit, leaving the core, or plug.

Use both hands to pick and place the fruit gently into the container, but fill the container only about 6–8 fruits deep to prevent the bottom fruits from being crushed.

Once the container is filled up, place it in a shaded place out of direct sunlight, with a paper cover to keep out insects. Do not use a plastic cover as it may keep in the heat and natural chemicals that speed up the ripening process.

Within half an hour of picking the fruit, take it inside and place it in a cool, dark place in order to reduce the heat and slow down the ripening process.

TOOLS FOR THE JOB

Pruner (for trimming)

MATERIALS

Containers

Sheets of paper or newspaper

vegetable directory

The interest in growing vegetables is probably greater now than it has been for many years, with more gardeners trying to create the ideal conditions for growing food, not out of obligation but as part of their own lifestyle.

VEGETABLE DESCRIPTIONS

VEGETABLES	PLANT TYPES	USES	PROPAGATION	COMMENTS
	Asparagus Herbaceous perennial that prefers a deep, free-draining soil.	Young edible shoots are produced in late spring and early summer.	By division of crowns that can crop for up to 20 years.	This plant will prove very useful for deterring some harmful eelworms.
	Beet Biennial plant grown as an annual. Likes full sun and a deep, fertile soil.	Swollen roots are eaten cooked, and raw leaves can also be eaten cooked.	Seed sown outdoors in spring and summer.	The leaves accumulate minerals, making them ideal for composting.
	Broad beans A hardy annual that is capable of growing outdoors over winter.	Edible seeds, young pods, and shoots are all eaten cooked.	Seeds sown outdoors in the autumn or spring.	Plant around gooseberry in order to discourage gooseberry sawflies.
	Brussels sprouts A biennial grown as an annual. Prefers a heavy, well-drained soil.	Young edible buds or shoot tips usually eaten cooked.	Seed sown under protection for spring transplanting.	Grow older cultivars that have a longer cropping season.
	Cabbage Biennial plant grown as an annual. Likes full sun and a deep, fertile soil.	Grown for their edible leaves, which are eaten either cooked or raw.	Seed sown under protection or outdoors all year round.	Very rich in vitamin C, especially when eaten raw.
	Carrot Biennial plant grown as an annual. Likes full sun and a deep, fertile soil.	Grown for their edible orange roots that can be eaten raw or cooked.	Seed sown in succession outdoors in the spring and summer.	Use the cultivar 'Flyaway' to avoid carrot rust flies.
	Cauliflower Grown as an annual, this plant prefers a warm, sheltered site.	Immature flowerheads and leaves are edible either cooked or raw.	Seeds sown outdoors in the spring and summer.	Grows well with garlic, onions, beets, and chard.
	Chard Biennial plant grown as an annual. Likes full sun and a deep, fertile soil.	Edible leaves and fleshy leaf stalks are eaten after they are cooked.	Seed sown in succession outdoors in the spring and summer.	Rich in sodium, potassium, and iron. Grows well with garlic, dill, and sage.
	Cucumber Grown as an annual in a warm, sheltered site.	Swollen edible fruits are eaten raw or cooked.	Seed sown under protection in the spring.	Grows well with peas, beans, beets, and carrots.
	Eggplant Grown as an annual, this plant prefers a warm, sheltered site.	Egg-shaped edible fruits that are eaten cooked or raw in salads.	Seed sown under protection in the spring.	Grows well with peas, thyme, and tarragon as companions.
	Garlic Perennial plant grown as an annual. Likes full sun and a deep, fertile soil.	Grown for their swollen leaf bases and leaves, which are eaten either raw or cooked.	Grown from bulb segments ("cloves") in the spring or autumn.	A natural medicine, this plant also deters aphids on surrounding crops.

VEGETABLE DESCRIPTIONS

VEGETABLES	PLANT TYPES	USES	PROPAGATION	COMMENTS
	Kale A biennial plant grown as an annual. Prefers a moist, well-drained soil.	Immature leaves and shoots are edible either raw or cooked.	Seeds sown outdoors in the autumn or spring.	A good source of vitamins E, C, iron, and calcium.
	Leek Biennial plant grown as an annual. Likes full sun and a deep, fertile soil.	Grown for their blanched leaf bases.	Sow seeds in the spring and summer for transplanting later.	Grown with carrots and onions, they help to deter rust flies.
	Lettuce Annual plant with a short life span. Prefers a moist, well-drained soil.	Grown for their edible leaves, eaten either raw or cooked.	Seeds sown outdoors in the spring, autumn, and summer.	Plant with chervil and dill to get some protection from aphids.
	Onion Biennial plant grown as an annual. Likes full sun and a deep, fertile soil.	Grown for their swollen leaf bases and leaves, eaten raw or cooked.	Seeds sown outdoors in the autumn or spring.	Grow seedlings under fine net or fleece to combat onion flies.
	Parsnip Biennial plant grown as an annual. Likes full sun and a deep, fertile soil.	Swollen roots are eaten cooked or raw or used as a sweetener.	Seeds sown outdoors in the spring and summer.	Highest sugar content of any vegetable and high mineral content.
	Peas An annual rambling plant. Prefers full sun and a deep, fertile soil.	Edible seeds and pods are usually cooked before eating.	Seeds sown outdoors in the spring and summer.	Roots can harness nitrogen, which will become available for other crops.
	Pepper Grown as an annual, this plant prefers a warm, sheltered site.	Large edible fruits that are eaten either cooked or raw in salads.	Seeds sown under protection in the spring.	Very rich in vitamin C, seeds and sap of some can be a skin irritant.
	Potato Perennial plant grown as an annual. Likes full sun and a deep, fertile soil.	Grown for their swollen stems ("tubers"), which are edible when cooked.	Propagation is by division of tubers planted in late spring.	Prevent potato scab by planting them on a bed of comfrey leaves.
	Pumpkin An annual plant that prefers full sun and a light, well-drained soil.	The leaves, fruits, and seeds can be used cooked or raw in many dishes.	Propagation is by seeds sown in the spring.	Pumpkin seeds are said to contain high levels of important minerals.
	Tomato Grown as an annual, this plant prefers a warm, sheltered site.	Round or plum-shaped edible fruits are eaten cooked or raw.	Seeds sown under protection in the spring.	Interplant with French marigolds to deter whiteflies.
	Turnip Biennial plant grown as an annual. Likes full sun and a deep, fertile soil.	Swollen roots are eaten cooked or raw and the leaves can be eaten when cooked.	Seeds sown outdoors in the spring and summer.	Provides small amounts of vitamin B and C. Grows well with peas.
	Zucchini Grown as an annual in a warm, sheltered site.	Swollen edible fruits are eaten raw or cooked.	Seeds sown under protection in the spring.	Grows well when placed alongside sweet corn.

salad vegetables

Celery

This vegetable is grown for its crisp, blanched leaf stalks that are available in white, pink, and red forms. The outer leaves are usually tough and stringy, and so should be discarded. Celery needs a deep, stone-free, well-drained, and fertile soil that has plenty of organic matter incorporated into it. Propagation is by seeds sown in trays or modules under protection from early spring onward, and transplanted quite close together in order to block out the light and help the blanching process as the plants mature approximately nine weeks later. Harvest celery by digging up the entire plant, starting from late summer onward. ❋ ❋ ❋ ❋ ❋ ❋ ❋

Yield: 20–26 lbs. per 10 ft. of row.

Lettuce

There are many forms of lettuce available, including many loose-leaf types that will tolerate most soils and growing conditions. Leaf color varies from pale green to reddish brown, which has both a decorative and edible value. Lettuce is grown from seeds, and harvesting can start about 12 weeks after planting, either as entire plants cut off at soil level or by pulling away the outer rows of leaves from large plants on a regular basis. Be sure to keep the plants well-watered in the last two weeks before harvesting, which is when they make their greatest increase in size. ❋ ❋ ❋ ❋ ❋ ❋

Yield: 3–6 lbs. per 10 ft. of row.

Radishes

These are grown for their swollen roots, which come in a wide range of colors, shapes, and sizes. If different types are grown, it is possible to have them available throughout the year. They are grown from seed thinly sown into drills that are $1/2$ in. deep and about 6 in. apart. To ensure continuity, sow the seeds in small batches at 10-day intervals so that there are always some ready for harvest. Most radishes will be ready for harvesting 14–21 days after sowing, and will be about 1 in. across at their widest point. ❋ ❋ ❋ ❋ ❋ ❋ ❋

Yield: 4$1/2$–10 lbs. per 11 ft. of row.

Arugula

This tender-looking plant is actually quite hardy. The leaves have a strong, tangy flavor. Sow the seed in succession at three-week intervals starting from midspring through early summer and keep them well-watered to promote rapid growth. To harvest the crop, remove individual leaves from the plants, or cut the plants down to about 1 in. above ground level and wait for them to resprout before cutting them again. Arugula can be eaten either raw or cooked. ❋ ❋ ❋ ❋ ❋ ❋

Yield: 3 lbs. per 10 ft. of row.

Spring onions

Spring onions have small, white stems and green leaves, and they are often put in salads. They are grown from seeds, which can be sown at two- to three-week intervals from March until June for continuous supplies both in summer and autumn. Hardier cultivars can be sown in August to provide an overwintering crop that will be ready for use the following spring. The best yields come from sowing in rows 4 in. apart, or they can be grown in strips 3 in. wide, with a gap of 6 in. between strips, aiming for 300 plants per square yard. Simply pull up the plants to harvest them. Because these plants crop very quickly, they can be sown between rows of slower-growing plants such as cauliflower. Harvest the crop of spring onions before the leaves of the cauliflower have spread sufficiently to block out the sunlight. ❋ ❋ ❋ ❋ ❋

Yield: 250–300 plants per square yard.

TOP LEFT *Grown for its edible green- or bronze-colored leaves, lettuce actually has little nutritional value.*

TOP RIGHT *Grown for their intense flavor, red-skinned radishes are more common, but there are also black-, purple-, green-, and yellow-skinned cultivars available.*

CENTER *For best flavor and texture, celery stems can be covered ("blanched") to keep them soft and tender.*

BOTTOM LEFT *Spring onions are harvested while immature, before the base of the stem has started to swell.*

BOTTOM RIGHT *Arugula leaves are rich in vitamin C and potassium.*

salad vegetables ❖ **167**

hardy vegetables

Beans (dwarf bush)

Also known as "string beans," these are grown for their tube-like, curved, green pods that are eaten whole. There are also yellow- and purple-podded cultivars. Sow seeds in double rows from late spring through midautumn at three-week intervals in order to ensure continuity. Start harvesting the pods when they are well-developed and about 4 in. long. They are ready when the pods can be cleanly snapped in half. Keep picking on a regular basis to encourage the plants to produce a heavier crop. Harvest from midsummer through to the very first autumn frosts, when the plants are actually killed off. ❀ ❀ ❀ ❀ ❀

Yield: 1¹/₂–2¹/₄ lbs. per plant.

Broccoli

Well-grown broccoli is very tasty eaten fresh and is also ideal for freezing. These plants grow back quickly, so start by cutting the central spike followed by the smaller spikes of the side shoots later. Seeds are sown individually into pots and transplanted outdoors, with many cultivars maturing within 12 weeks of sowing. Water keeps the plants growing rapidly and producing a good crop, with the critical times being the first month after sowing and a three-week period immediately before cropping commences. ❀ ❀ ❀ ❀ ❀ ❀ ❀

Yield: 1 lb. per plant.

Cabbage

There are many types of cabbage available, which means that it is possible to have fresh cabbage all year round. All types are cultivated in much the same way, but seed sowing and planting varies according to the time of year, the cultivars chosen, and the time taken to reach maturity. When the cabbages have developed a good solid heart, they are ready for harvesting. Using a sharp knife, cut through the main stem to remove all of the heart and a few outer leaves, leaving the stem and oldest leaves in the soil. ❀ ❀ ❀ ❀ ❀ ❀ ❀

Yield: 1–4 lbs. per plant.

Carrots

A popular root vegetable needing a deep, stone-free, well-drained, fertile soil. Carrots are propagated from seeds thinly sown in place from late spring to midsummer in shallow drills 6–8 in. apart, which are thinned out later. Early cultivars are ready eight weeks after sowing, and main-crop sowings take 10–12 weeks to mature. Harvest early crops by easing them out with a fork and then pulling by hand. Larger carrots are dug up with a fork for immediate use, freezing, or storing through winter. Control weeds by hoeing between the rows. ❀ ❀ ❀ ❀ ❀ ❀ ❀

Yield: 20–26 lbs. per 10 ft. of row.

Cauliflower

It is possible to have cauliflower ready for harvest for most of the year, from early spring through midwinter. Spacing will vary depending on when the plants are being grown and harvested. Usually, the later the planting, the larger the cauliflower will grow and the greater the space needed for each plant. Seeds sown individually into small pots are ready to be transplanted when four leaves have developed. They are ready for harvesting when the leaves start to open, showing the curd beneath. The curd is removed by cutting through the main stem with a sharp knife. Cauliflower needs to be protected from birds, especially when the plants are young. Wood pigeons, in particular, will search out cauliflower and completely devastate the crop if they are allowed to. ❀ ❀ ❀ ❀ ❀ ❀ ❀

Yield: 1–2³/₄ lbs. per plant.

TOP LEFT *Broccoli is grown for its green, immature flower stalks and heads, which become inedible when the flowers are fully open.*

TOP RIGHT *A popular way to eat broad beans is to harvest them while immature and eat them whole.*

CENTER *Cauliflower is grown for its creamy-white, immature flower heads, which are partially hidden and protected by the outer leaves.*

BOTTOM LEFT *Grown for their orange tap roots, carrots come in a variety of shapes— from long and narrow to almost globe-shaped. Usually the younger the carrots are when picked, the sweeter the flavor.*

BOTTOM RIGHT *The type, strength of flavor, and color of cabbage leaves will vary depending on the time of year.*

hardy vegetables ❁ 169

Garlic

This hardy vegetable, with its strong, characteristic flavor, is easier to grow than most gardeners realize. Used as a flavoring in a range of cooked foods and salads, it also has antiseptic qualities. There are white- and purple-skinned cultivars. Propagate the plant by splitting the bulbs into individual segments ("cloves") and push these base first into the soil. Garlic bulbs should be lifted gently with a digging fork and dried as soon as the leaves start to turn yellow. The bulbs can be stored under cool, dry conditions for up to 10 months.

❀ ❀ ❀ ❀ ❀ ❀ ❀ ❀

Yield: an average bulb weighs about 3¹/₂ oz.

Onions

Bulb onions are grown as annual plants with the brown- or yellow-skinned cultivars being the most popular. They grow well in dry conditions, have a long growing season, and are grown from seeds sown in late summer or early spring into a well-drained, fertile soil, which should have been deeply cultivated beforehand. Onions are ready for harvesting when the leaves turn yellow and the tops bend over. Lift the bulbs gently using a digging fork and allow the bulbs to dry naturally before storing them. ❀ ❀ ❀ ❀ ❀

Yield: an average bulb weighs about 4¹/₂–6¹/₄ oz.

Peas

These plants are grown for their seeds, which are produced in either green or purple pods. The green pods are produced from the white-flowered cultivars, and purple pods come from purple-flowered types. They can be eaten fresh or stored dry for later use. Seeds are sown in situ into broad, flat-bottomed drills from early spring to early summer. As soon as two pairs of leaves develop, introduce a support system around the plants to get a higher yield. Start harvesting when the pods are swollen but before they are packed with seeds. Pick them regularly by pulling the pod downward away from the plant.

❀ ❀ ❀ ❀ ❀ ❀ ❀ ❀ ❀

Yield: about 1–2³/₄ lbs. per plant.

Potatoes

This versatile vegetable is a staple for many. It has to be cooked, but can be eaten hot or cold. "Potato seed" is the term used for young tubers that are planted to produce the next crop, but they are really stem tubers, not seeds. Plant the tubers about 8 in. deep, and earth up the base of each potato stem when they are 8–10 in. high, to cover the bottom 4–5 in. of stem. The usual method of harvesting potatoes is to dig into the ridge of earth in which they are growing with a garden fork. Always start by digging under the ridge of earth, to avoid stabbing and damaging the tubers.

❀ ❀ ❀ ❀ ❀ ❀ ❀ ❀ ❀

Yield: about 1¹/₂–2³/₄ lbs. per plant.

Swiss chard

Swiss chard is grown for its large, brightly colored, succulent, glossy leaves, which can grow up to 18 in. long and 8 in. wide. The leaf stalks resemble rhubarb stalks, and the leaves range in color from deep green to copper-green or red. Plants are produced from seed sown in drills any time from early spring through until midsummer. The crop is usually ready for cutting 12 weeks after sowing, and will often occupy the ground for almost a whole year. Harvest by cutting off the outer leaves at soil level. Keep this crop well-watered, especially in the early stages of growth. If the young plants are allowed to become too dry, they have a tendency to stop growing leaves and produce a flowering stem, before setting seeds. ❀ ❀ ❀ ❀ ❀ ❀

Yield: about 1 lb. per plant.

TOP LEFT *One of the hardiest vegetables to be grown in the garden, garlic has a strong, distinctive flavor and is used more for flavoring than as a true edible vegetable.*

TOP RIGHT *Although grown mainly for their green or yellow seeds, some types of peas are eaten whole with both pods and seeds.*

CENTER LEFT *Onions are actually the swollen stems of plants, and not only can the outer skin color vary from deep red through orange and yellow to white, the flavor can also vary in strength.*

CENTER RIGHT *Swiss chard is a highly productive vegetable that can be harvested continuously as the outer leaves mature.*

BOTTOM *One of the most versatile vegetables available, potatoes can be cooked in any number of ways. The flesh color is usually yellow, cream, or white.*

hardy vegetables ❀ 171

tender vegetables

Cucumbers

Grown for their swollen fruits, which are eaten raw, these tropical plants do not tolerate low temperatures, so a frost-free environment is essential. These plants will grow well in a loamless compost, such as a growing bag. Propagation is by seeds sown individually into 3-in. pots, under protection in midspring, and the seedlings are ready for planting into the growing site when they are 1 ft. high. Harvesting can begin about 16 weeks after the seed has germinated; the fruits are cut from the plant leaving a short stalk of about 1 in. on the fruit. ✿ ✿ ✿ ✿ ✿ ✿ ✿ ✿ ✿ ✿

Yield: about 20 fruits per plant.

Eggplant

This dense, bushy plant is grown for its egg-shaped fruits, which are usually a blackish-purple and which add both a rich texture and flavor to many dishes. They prefer a warm, sheltered spot and a deep, fertile soil. They will grow well in containers, provided they are well-fed and watered. Plants are grown from seeds sown directly into small pots under protection in midspring, and are transplanted as the first flowers open. Harvest can start about 16 weeks after transplanting. Remove the vegetables by cutting the stalk above the top of the fruits when they are fully swollen and firm with a smooth skin. ✿ ✿ ✿ ✿ ✿ ✿ ✿ ✿ ✿ ✿

Yield: 4–5 fruits per plant.

Peppers

Grown under protection for their red, yellow, and orange bell-shaped fruits, sweet bell peppers have a distinctive flavor that becomes sweeter as the fruits ripen. Propagation is by seeds sown into pots in midspring, and young plants are ready for transplanting 10 weeks after germination. Peppers prefer a deep soil, but grow well in containers such as growing bags or

pots, and need staking for support. Harvesting the green fruits starts about 14 weeks after transplanting, slightly later for the colored fruits. These are harvested when they are fully swollen and firm, by cutting the stalk from the top of the fruit. ✿ ✿ ✿ ✿ ✿ ✿ ✿ ✿ ✿

Yield: about 6 fruits per plant.

Squash and zucchini

These cylindrical fruits come in a range of colors from white and yellow to green, and have a wide range of uses in hot and cold dishes. They are trailing plants, which grow very well in containers such as a growing bag. They are propagated by seeds sown individually into 3-in. pots under cover in midspring, and the seedlings are ready to be planted into the growing site when they have three leaves. Harvesting can start about 13 weeks after seed germination.This process involves the fruits being cut from the plant, leaving a short stalk of about 1 in. on the fruit. ✿ ✿ ✿

Yield: Squash 5–6/Zucchini 15–20 fruits per plant.

Tomatoes

This vegetable can produce red, orange, yellow, pink, and even orange- and yellow-striped fruit when ripe to be used raw or cooked. For sheltered cultivation, individual seeds are sown in 4-in. pots indoors by late spring, and are transplanted as the first flowers open. They are trained up support stakes, making closer spacing possible. When five fruit trusses have formed, remove the growing stem tip just above the top truss to encourage even development of the fruits. Pick the fruits as they ripen and this will encourage others to ripen. Try to avoid growing tomato plants in an area where potatoes have grown in previous years—as being close relatives they are both prone to the same pests and diseases. ✿ ✿ ✿ ✿ ✿ ✿ ✿ ✿ ✿ ✿

Yield: about 5–10 lbs. per plant.

TOP LEFT *Eggplants, with their dark glossy skins, look more like decorations than food. Once the skin has lost its shine, the flesh develops a bitter taste.*

TOP RIGHT *Sweet peppers come in a range of colors and can be eaten when green, but if they are allowed to ripen and change color, the flavor improves and becomes sweeter.*

CENTER *Possibly the most common fruiting vegetable, the tomato has a variety of uses in a wide range of dishes and recipes.*

BOTTOM LEFT *The fruits of squash and zucchini come in a wide range of shapes and sizes. Remove any male flowers or the fruit will have a very bitter flesh.*

BOTTOM RIGHT *Most modern cucumber cultivars do not need pollinating to produce fruit, but if they are left on the plant for too long after reaching maturity, the fruits will develop a tough skin.*

harvesting and storing vegetables

It is important that only the best of the crop is selected for storage, although produce with some marking or slight damage can still be used immediately. Any parts of the plant that are brown, wilted (when they are not supposed to be), bruised, or that show any signs of pest-and-disease damage should not be stored because these problems may be transferred to the healthy plants in storage.

The harvesting and storage of vegetables will depend on a number of factors, particularly the climate and the type of vegetable. In cool climates, where crops mature fairly slowly, it is possible to leave them growing and harvest them only when required, especially since many are not eaten until they reach maturity. Others, such as salad vegetables that are harvested while semimature, are cut while they are still young.

The biggest problem, especially with leafy vegetables or those that are harvested when young, is one of short-term storage; that is keeping the soft, edible tissue fresh and palatable until it is eaten.

Some vegetables, such as beans, cabbage, chilies, garlic, squash, onions, peas, and tomatoes will keep quite well if they are stored under dry conditions and allowed to dry slowly in a cool, frost-free place, but others will need to be kept in airtight containers.

AUTHOR'S TIP:
Drying vegetables

Vegetables can be dried outdoors in warm, dry, windy weather conditions for a period of about 24–36 hours.

CLOCKWISE FROM TOP LEFT

Harvesting leafy vegetables

Start in the morning, while it is still cool, and with a sharp knife, cut through the stem just above ground level and trim off any damaged or very dirty leaves.

Wash the vegetables in cold water, and leave them plunged in very cold water for 30 minutes after they have been harvested. This will lower their temperature dramatically and prolong their keeping qualities.

Remove the vegetables from the water, and allow them to drain.

Store the vegetables in clear, open plastic bags and leave the bags in a cool, damp place until required.

Drying vegetables

Start by carefully removing the bean pods from the plant, using both your hands.

Place the bean pods in a tray or in a container of your choice. Allow them to dry in a dry, cool room.

When the pods start to split, remove the seeds for storage.

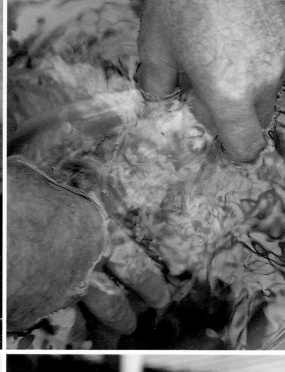

TOOLS FOR THE JOB

1 sharp knife

MATERIALS

Clear plastic bags

Trays or containers

harvesting and storing herbs *The traditional method of harvesting and storing herbs is by cutting and drying them. More recently, freezing has become equally popular as a means of storing herbs for use over the long periods when they are out of season. This method is particularly recommended for both parsley and basil.*

When harvesting herbs, the most important factor is to cut them with sharp tools—anything that crushes or bruises the stem will make the herbs bleed sap, lose much of their flavor, and possibly turn moldy. Only cut the freshest, leafiest, upper stems from the plant. The best time to harvest is in the morning, when the herbs are still full of moisture, but after the dew has dried off. This process can also act as a pruning session; it will help to keep the plant compact and bushy. Do not cut any leaves or stems that are brown, wilted, damaged, or showing signs of pests and diseases. To preserve the flavor and for sanitary purposes, store the dry herbs in dark glass jars with screw-top lids.

While it is normally the leaves of the plants that are collected and saved, other parts of the plant may be used, including stems, roots, and seeds. Perhaps the most commonly eaten herb root is the horseradish. Angelica, dill, and fennel have their seeds harvested as well as other parts of the plant.

Flowers can also be used not only for their flavor but as a decoration. Some, such as nasturtium, are used fresh, while others, such as borage, can be frozen in ice cubes for use later, in cool summer drinks.

AUTHOR'S TIP:
Freezing herbs

Once the herbs have frozen they can be stored in plastic bags and the ice-cube trays reused.

CLOCKWISE FROM TOP LEFT

Harvesting and drying herbs

Cut the herbs and make up small bunches of clean, dry stems, the number varying according to their thickness. For instance, bundle rosemary up to 10 stalks at a time, and for bay leaves, dry separate branches.

Hang them upside down in a dry, dark, well-ventilated place. The temperature should be between 70° F–90° F, for 5–14 days until they are dry and crisp.

When the herbs are totally dry, remove the leaves from the stems by rubbing them through your hands. Place them in dark, airtight glass jars. Label the jars with the name of the herb and the date of harvest, so that they can be used in order of freshness.

Harvesting and freezing herbs

Collect young tender shoots and keep them out of direct sunlight so they stay cool and fresh.

Wash the herbs thoroughly in cold water before dicing them into small sections using a sharp knife or pruner.

Place the chopped herbs into the compartments of an ice-cube tray and fill each compartment with water. Place the ice-cube trays in the freezer.

TOOLS FOR THE JOB

1 pruner

Rubber bands

MATERIALS

Dark, airtight glass jars

Ice-cube trays

harvesting flowers

Many gardeners face a dilemma when it comes to harvesting flowers. Some prefer to see their flowers in the garden where they feel they belong, while others prefer to brighten up rooms inside with displays of their best blooms, in order to enjoy them more fully.

ABOVE *Most flowers intended for drying must be picked or cut when they are about two-thirds open; they will continue to open.*

BELOW LEFT *Careful handling is crucial because bruised or damaged flowers will lose water too quickly, and molds will often develop in the damaged plant tissue.*

BELOW RIGHT *Cut flowers should be sorted, bunched, and hung quickly so they can dry at a steady rate and keep their natural color.*

Certainly both flowers and leaves, cut and skillfully arranged, bring brightness into any room and often provide a focal point, drawing the eye.

CUTTING   Flowers last much longer when they are harvested from the garden in early morning or evening when the air is relatively cool and the flowers have plenty of water, so they are less likely to wilt immediately.

Always cut the stems with sharp implements—a knife, a pruner, or sharp shears. Clean cuts, at an angle of about 45 degrees, will cause less bruising of the plant tissue and will also aid the uptake of water. When the flowers are cut in the evening, they can be plunged into cold water as soon as possible after cutting and remain in water overnight to be fresh for use the following day. If possible, plunge the stems to their full length in water, and keep as many leaves as possible on the stems until the flowers are being prepared for display.

PREPARATION   Some blooms will last for long periods in water without a great deal of preparation, while others will benefit from extra treatment. For all flowers, strip away any leaves that will be underwater in the vase or container, or they may soon begin to decay and smell very unpleasant.

The stems of plants like roses and chrysanthemums are very woody and this may impede the uptake of water. This particular type of stem can have the bottom 2 in. either split with a sharp knife or crushed with a hammer or similar heavy object. Other stems that have trouble taking up water (particularly those of plants that bleed), usually respond to having the bottom 1 in. of the stem plunged in boiling water for up to one minute, before transferring them to a deep container filled with warm water. Allow them to recover for two to three hours before placing them in the vase of your choice.

Hollow-stemmed plants can be quite a problem, since they tend to develop airlocks that prevent the uptake of water. This can be overcome by either tipping the flower so that the stem is facing upward, slowly filling the cavity with water and then plugging the base with tissue paper. Or you may prick a needle through the stem about 1 in. below the lowest flower in order to prevent the airlock.

Once all the blooms have been carefully prepared and arranged, a chemical preparation may be added to the water in the vase in order to prolong the life of the flowers. These can be commercial mixtures, although some people prefer to make their own cocktails. Charcoal, aspirin, sugar, or lemonade are all among those most commonly used. Finally, top off the water in the vase on a daily basis, and make sure to change the water completely every five days or so.

ABOVE *Dried flowers provide the backbone of indoor displays throughout the winter when fresh flowers are expensive and their availability is limited.*

BELOW *Plants can look stunning when they are in flower, but they can also provide a very dramatic display if the seedheads are cut and used for dried-flower arrangements.*

harvesting and drying flowers *Many*

gardeners save flowers to preserve and use in dry displays to brighten up their house during winter. Even if they have not intentionally grown plants with this in mind, there may be plants already in their garden that can be used. Although the flower heads will often dry naturally if left on the plant, the weather will take its toll, and these look very shabby compared with those cut and dried when at their peak.

Ideally, flowers should be cut just before they become fully open, on a fine, dry day. Do not collect them when it is damp or if they are still covered with morning dew, as they will become moldy and discolored, and will not dry

properly. Most flowers can be air dried but some are more difficult than others. It is a slow process, often taking up to several weeks.

The best method is to hang the flowers upside down in small, loose bunches (tightly tied at the base), in a dry, well-ventilated place away from direct sunlight, or the flowers will fade. The remaining leaves will soon dry and the larger ones shrivel. Once this happens, the bunches should be tapped gently until these leaves have fallen. The bunches can then be removed from the drying area and stored by hanging them in a cool, dry place, such as a garage or shed, until they are needed.

AUTHOR'S TIP:
Microwave drying

Some plants can be dried in a microwave oven, which is very quick: a rose flower dries in about 2 minutes 50 seconds, compared with one week with air drying. However, flowers become more brittle when dried this way.

CLOCKWISE FROM TOP LEFT

Start cutting when the flowers are half to three-quarters open. This will compensate for the flowers opening further as they are drying. Cut the stems with a sharp knife or a pruner, making a sloping cut through the stem or flower stalk. Start cutting only when the surface of the whole plant (including the flowers) is totally dry to prevent mold from developing.

As they are cut, lay the flower heads and stems in a dry container, such as a cardboard box, but do not fill the box too full or the bottom flowers will become crushed and bruised.

Working on a bench or table, sort through the flower stalks, removing any large leaves from the bottom half of the stalk.

Grade and sort the stems for size and length, gathering between 5–10 stems together into a group.

Tie these stems firmly with a rubber band. Do not use string; it loosens up as the stems dry and shrink.

Hang the complete bunches in a dry, cool, dark place with good ventilation, and leave them for 2–4 weeks, depending on the plants being dried and how dry the atmosphere is.

TOOLS FOR THE JOB

1 sharp knife or pruner

MATERIALS

Dry containers
(such as cardboard boxes)

Elastic bands

autumn
SHUTDOWN

The arrival of autumn signals that the growing season is drawing to a close for a large number of plants. Shorter days trigger big changes for deciduous, woody plants as they begin to shut down for the winter by shedding their leaves and getting prepared for cold weather. Annuals die off with the first frosts, and herbaceous perennials appear to be dead as their tops die away, although their parts underground are filled with food ready for the new tops, which will reappear the following spring.

Autumn indicates a beginning in the garden as well as an end. It is the time to look back over the growing season, to use its successes and failures as aids to planning ahead for the next season. Successes can be built upon, and any failures learned from and rectified—or at least not repeated. New plants that were introduced but did not work can be dug up and either disposed of, traded with a friend or neighbor, or given a second chance elsewhere in the garden. Do not be afraid to move them around to another position—as long as they are transplanted carefully and watered well, they will survive the move and may even grow much better than they did before. Ordering seeds and new plants can be done at this time of year while the performance of last season's crops can still be assessed, and crop rotations can be planned and organized for next year's vegetable garden. This is an ideal time to plan new hard landscape features and planting designs. You can also take the time now to grow the same plants but in a different way.

Even parts of the plant that have died and been discarded have a purpose. Fallen leaves, shredded prunings, and other plant trimmings all have a future role within the garden, as they are gathered up and recycled. Composted, they will provide part of the food system that will feed next year's plants. The plants might be resting but the gardening still goes on. This is definitely not a quiet time.

RIGHT *The glorious autumn leaf colors of this Japanese maple are produced as the plant extracts nutrients from the leaves to store in the woody stems.*

putting the garden to bed

As the plants in the garden gradually start to shut down for the winter, the best thing a gardener can do is to help this natural process, rather than trying to fight it. A general tidying up of the garden is usually carried out at this time: trimming back straggling plants, digging up others that will go indoors for winter protection, and raking and collecting leaves to be used for making excellent compost and mulching material.

During this time, the lawn will require less mowing, and when the grass is cut, the blade setting should be high to leave the grass longer and protect the roots from frost. Fall lawn feed, which is high in potassium and phosphates, will slow down the growth rate and also toughen the grass, making it hardier so it can withstand the cold weather. If there is a lot of moss in the lawn, moss killer should be applied now while the moss is still growing. Moss tends to be worse in the autumn when fallen leaves collect on the grass and block out the light. If moss persists, the pH of the soil should be tested, as it tends to be more of a problem on acidic soils. Adding a little lime could be more long-lasting than a lot of moss killer.

BELOW *As autumn progresses, the woodland garden is enriched with a tapestry of greens, yellows, reds, and oranges, in a far greater range of shades than any painter's palette.*

Mulching can be beneficial at this time of year. A mulch will keep the soil warmer around newly transplanted trees and shrubs by trapping the summer heat. This will encourage new roots to form and help the plant establish quickly, even though the top growth may have already shut down for the winter. Mulches will also protect the base (or "crown") of plants that are to be overwintered outside. In mild areas, fuchsias, dahlias, and some chrysanthemums can be protected in this way.

Winter storage of many root vegetables starts now, and you should prioritize those that are the most frost-sensitive or are on wet soils. Where the soils are lighter and free-draining, a mulch of straw over crops left in the ground will often protect them from cold up until Christmas.

Newly planted broad-leaved evergreens and conifers may need some wind protection as the weather becomes worse. A mesh screen will help stop the leaves from drying out and turning brown in cold, windy weather. When herbaceous borders are being tidied and old dead leaves removed, some of the plants can be lifted and divided, particularly those that have been left undisturbed for over three years.

Plants that are growing in containers can be moved closer together as a means of helping to protect them from the frost, and some form of wrapping should be made ready to use, so that it is readily available for covering the plants in case the weather suddenly turns very cold.

As you are putting the garden to bed, you should definitely use this opportunity to plan for the spring. Plant spring-flowering bulbs for a good show early in the coming year as you are working your way around the borders in the garden.

ABOVE LEFT *Schizostylis ('Kaffir lily') flowers in late summer and early autumn. Its appearance is a mixed blessing, as it is a sign that the growing season is ending.*

ABOVE *Even dead and dying flowers can have their attractions. The flower heads of* Helenium *'Moerheim Beauty,' coated with a dusting of frost, provide interest on an autumn morning.*

BELOW *At the end of the season, hostas die down to form a tangled carpet of browns and yellows.*

ABOVE *In autumn, tie in any loose, flapping growths to protect them during winter winds, especially those on plants with long stems.*

OPPOSITE PAGE *Water in the garden has an added value when the vivid autumn leaf colors are clearly reflected on a sunny day.*

BELOW *Newly planted conifers and evergreens will benefit from wind protection during their first winter in a new site.*

Cutting back, training, and tying

Often the tallest and most vigorous plants are the ones that suffer most during the autumn and winter months, and most of their injuries come as a result of wind damage. Young trees, which are still staked and tied, will need a thorough checking over in late summer or early autumn to make sure they are secure for winter. Replace a stake (if it is still needed by the plant) if it is rotten, split, or broken. Make sure never to just add another, smaller stake to the damaged one as this will make matters worse.

All ties fixing a tree to a stake should be checked to ensure that they are not damaged or broken. The tension will need verifying as well, to make sure it is tight enough to hold the tree without rubbing it, but is not so tight that it actually strangles the stem.

Tall plants with long flexible stems, such as clematis, climbing and rambling roses, as well as all of the cane fruits, will need attention. The majority of these plants should have been pruned earlier in the year and will consequently have produced a fair amount of new shoot growth that will need to be tied to a supporting frame. If there is no supporting frame in place, the long branches can be tied together to form a column of shoots that will protect one another until they can be tied to a support. If these shoots are left to flap about freely against one another, or against their support, a considerable amount of damage can be inflicted during only a few hours of windy weather. Stems that either rub together or become split and cracked can later succumb to frost damage, and can provide the perfect overwintering site for pests and diseases.

Tall bush and shrub roses can also fall victim to the strong winds of autumn, especially on exposed sites. As the wind rocks the plant, the main stem of the plant will form a funnel-shaped depression around it in the soil which can fill with water and lead to waterlogging and rotting. In a really cold winter this water freezes, and if the stem continues to rock, its bark is damaged by knocking against the ice, often resulting in the death of the whole plant. There are two ways to cope with this problem. Either give the plants extra shelter with some form of screening, or cut the rose stems down to about half of their length to reduce the wind resistance.

Other plants, such as buddleia and mallow, which tend to put on a lot of rampant growth but do not like autumn pruning because their new growth is very easily damaged by frost, can also suffer from wind damage in a considerable way. The best approach with these particular plants is to reduce the top growth by at least one-third. No harm will actually be done if any new growth is damaged in the winter, because these plants will be pruned lower in the spring anyway.

Preventive measures

As the growing season draws to a close, and the gardener begins to consider his or her plans for the coming year, some of these future plans can be acted upon almost immediately. Many of the pests and diseases that have plagued the plants in the growing season that has just ended will also be making winter plans in order to survive.

Insects, such as aphids, lay eggs with specially toughened shells to aid winter survival, and a large number of fungi produce overwintering spores that will emerge the following spring. It is possible to act against these potential problems in late summer and early autumn in order to reduce the primary populations causing harm the subsequent year.

Diseases—such as black spot and mildew on roses, and peach leaf curl, which attacks members of the plum and cherry family—are only visible when they are active in the summer and can only be effectively controlled at that time of year with frequent sprays. However, by using a "winter wash" spray in the autumn just before leaf fall, it is possible to kill or damage many of the overwintering spores so that those that are not killed outright will die when they are exposed to the winter cold.

ABOVE *As the days get shorter, some garden residents are busy stocking their own pantries.*

BELOW *This euonymus can only really display its attractive fruits once all the leaves have fallen away.*

These same chemicals will often work very effectively against aphid eggs as well. It is important to spray not just the plants concerned but the surrounding soil and, in the case of climbing plants, any supports such as fences, since pests and diseases may also hibernate in these specific places. This cleansing process will leave the plants and surrounding areas relatively clean for the following spring when the new growth starts.

As part of the cleaning-up process, it is a good policy to rake up infected leaves and destroy them rather than composting them, in order to reduce the spore population for the following spring. Dipping bamboo canes in a mild disinfectant solution can kill off eggs and spores that may overwinter in cracks and crevices only to reinfect the plants during the following year.

For a more organic approach, create some overwintering positions where beneficial insects, such as hoverflies, lacewings, and ladybugs, can hibernate and emerge to feed on aphids the following spring. Leaving piles of prunings to provide winter shelter for visitors, such as hedgehogs, will help to give slugs a hard time when they start emerging the next year.

Autumn digging can also be useful—not only is it good to let winter frosts break down heavy soils, but turning over the topsoil will bury weeds and crop debris that may be infested with insect pests or disease. Turning and breaking the soil can expose food items, such as slug eggs, to foraging birds, therefore reducing the population for next spring. Barriers, such as bands around the stems of trees, are an effective way of preventing insect pests, such as the female winter moth, from climbing up into apple trees to lay their eggs. Unfortunately, this method is not effective against other troublesome moths, like the codling moth and the tortrix moth, because the females can fly in and bypass the bands.

Looking over your achievements

Every growing season is different because both the weather and temperature vary continuously, making seasons warmer or colder, later or earlier, and wetter or drier than we may expect. In response to these variations, different plants will perform well in different years, because they were slightly better suited to the prevailing conditions of that year.

Dealing with these factors and learning how to even out their effects means that the gardener must rely on experience, skill, and knowledge of the plants and the seasons to help redress the balance and give a degree of consistency. Luck will also play a small part in this, of course.

It is important to look at the garden and the growing season as a whole, but also to examine individual plants or particular cultivars to analyze their performance. If the display or crop has not lived up to your expectations, try to find a reason; there may not always be one, but this will only become clear once you have examined it closely. Be ruthless if necessary, and get rid of plants that consistently underachieve. Space in the garden is limited, and so it should only be occupied by plants that can earn their keep.

For short-term crops, such as vegetables and decorative annuals, the disappointments can be quite easily dealt with—try another cultivar with a higher resistance to the problem, whether it is cultural, or a pest or disease. Long-term plants are a different prospect altogether. Soft fruits, such as strawberries, have a cropping life of about three years before they go into decline, and should be replaced on a rotational basis. Bush and cane fruits may crop for up to 20 years, but often start to decline long before, as they

ABOVE *Some plants have a short but very productive season and often produce edible fruit right up until the first frosts of autumn.*

BELOW *Clusters of blackberries ripen over several weeks, providing a natural succession of fruit that can be picked numerous times.*

BELOW RIGHT *Black currant bushes produce heavy crops of fruit, but over a short period, so often the only way to prevent excessive waste is to preserve some fruit for later use.*

become infected with virus diseases. These are transmitted by aphids and other sap-sucking insects. Since the disease causes a gradual decline in growth and fruit production, the poor performance is less obvious at first.

Most gardeners are unable to resist introducing new plants into their garden and, regardless of how overcrowded an area of the garden may have become, can always find room for "just one more." It is only by trying new or different plants that gardeners can find a selection of plants that are best suited for their own soil and situation. If you are unsure of which plants to grow, do not limit yourself to just looking back at what has already grown well in your own garden—look to see what is doing well in surrounding gardens and draw inspiration from those, too.

Regardless of how past growing seasons have been, try not to take the garden—or the plants growing in it—for granted. The soil, in particular, is the gardener's raw material. It lasts far longer than any one plant—or any one gardener for that matter—but without it you can achieve very little. It must be cared for and managed well to give good results. Remember, you only get out of a garden what you put into it: Feed the soil, and the soil will, in turn, feed the plants you grow.

ABOVE *Growing plants is often experimental, so record observations to ensure that any mistakes can be rectified and not repeated.*

BELOW *Mixed flower and vegetable borders often leave some color in the flower beds after the flowers have died for the winter.*

putting the garden to bed ❀ 191

glossary

Acclimatization (acclimation) Adjusting plants to different conditions (usually cooler) than those in which they are growing.

Aerate (soil) Loosening soil by physical or mechanical means to allow the penetration of air—as when using a tined fork to aerate the lawn.

Alkaline A substance (soil) with a pH value of 7.0 or higher.

Annual A plant that completes its reproduction cycle in one year.

Apex The tip of a shoot or branch.

Apical bud The uppermost bud in the growing point of a stem (also known as the "terminal bud").

Axil Where the leaf or branch joins the main stem of a plant.

Bark A protective layer of cells on the outer surface of the roots and stems of woody plants.

Base dressing An application of fertilizer or organic matter.

incorporated into the soil prior to planting or sowing.

Bed system A system of growing vegetables in closely spaced rows to form blocks of plants, thus reducing the area given over to paths.

Bedding plants Plants arranged in mass displays (beds) to form a colorful and temporary display.

Biennial A plant that completes its growing cycle in two growing seasons. It germinates and produces roots and leaves in its first year, then flowers and produces seeds before dying in the second year.

Biennial bearing A plant that slips into a habit of producing fruit on a two-year cycle.

Blanch Either to plunge sections of a plant in hot water or to exclude light from sections of a plant to keep the tissues soft and supple.

Bleeding The excessive flow of sap from spring-pruned plants.

Bolt The premature flowering and seed production of a cropping plant.

Branch A shoot that grows directly from the main stem of a woody plant.

Brassica A member of the cabbage family (cruciferae).

Broadcasting The technique of spreading fertilizer or seeds randomly.

Bud union The point where a cultivar is budded onto a rootstock.

Budding A propagation technique that is used to join two or more plants together.

Bulb A storage organ consisting of thick, fleshy leaves arranged on a compressed stem that is found below soil level.

Calcicole A plant that prefers a soil that is alkaline (pH 7.0+), usually a limey soil.

Calcifuge A plant that prefers a soil that is acidic (pH 7.0-), usually a peaty or organic soil.

Callus The plant tissue that forms to protect a cut or wounded surface.

Chilling A period of low temperature (usually 36° F) required by plants during dormancy to stimulate flower development.

Chipping Cutting bulbs into small sections to propagate them.

Climber A self-supporting plant capable of growing vertically.

Cloche A small, clear or opaque (glass or plastic) portable structure used for protecting plants.

Cold frame A low, clear, portable, or permanent structure used for protecting plants.

Companion planting Growing certain plant combinations close together to overcome pest and disease problems organically.

Compost Either a potting media made to a standard formula, which can be loam- or peat-based, or well-rotted organic matter such as garden waste.

Conifer A classification of plants that have naked ovules often borne in cones and narrow needle-like foliage.

Conservatory An ornamental, glass- or plastic-clad structure used for growing plants under controlled and protected conditions.

Corm An underground modified stem forming a storage organ.

Crop rotation A system of moving crops in a planned cycle in order to improve growth and help control pests and disease.

Crown The growing point of a herbaceous perennial oiginating at soil level.

Cultivar A plant form that originated in cultivation rather than having been found growing naturally in the wild.

Cutting A portion of a plant that is specifically used for propagation purposes.

Deadheading The deliberate removal of dead flower heads or seed-bearing fruits.

Debudding Removal of unwanted buds to produce fewer, but much larger flowers.

Deep beds A method of growing plants (usually vegetables) in a deeply cultivated bed that has organic matter incorporated into it.

Division A method of propagation used to increase the number of plants by splitting them up into smaller units.

Dormancy A period of reduced growth through the winter.

Drainage The free movement of surplus water through the soil/compost.

Drill A narrow, straight line into which seeds are sown.

Dry storage A method of storing edible plants in readiness for use.

Earthing up Mounding up the soil around the base of a plant.

Fertile A soil rich in nutrients and biological life.

Fertilizer An organic or inorganic compound full of nutrients, used to help plants grow.

Force Inducing plants to start growing earlier than usual.

Formative pruning A pruning method carried out on young plants to establish a desired plant shape and branch structure.

Fruit set The successful formation of fruits.

Fungicide A chemical used to control fungal disease.

Garden fabric (fleece) Light, woven, geotextile material used to protect plants from frost or used as a barrier against insect pests.

Grafting A propagation method involving the joining of two or more separate plants together.

Germination The process by which a seed develops into a plant.

Greenhouse A glass- or plastic structure that is used for growing plants under controlled and protected conditions.

Ground cover The term used to describe low-growing plants.

Half-hardy A plant that can tolerate low temperatures but is killed by frost.

Hardening off The method of adjusting plants to different conditions (usually cooler) than those in which they are growing.

Hardy A plant that can tolerate temperatures below freezing without protection.

Herbaceous A nonwoody plant with an annual top and a perennial root system or storage organ.

Herbicide A chemical that is used to kill weeds.

Hoeing A method of shallow cultivation that is used to kill weed seedlings.

Humus The organic residue of decayed organic material.

Inorganic A man-made chemical compound (one that does not contain carbon).

Insecticide A chemical that is used to kill insects.

Intercrop A short-term crop grown between other crops.

Irrigation A general term used for the systemized application of water to plants.

Lateral A side shoot that arises from an axillary bud.

Layering A propagation technique in which roots are formed on a stem before it is detached from the parent plant.

Leaching The loss of nutrients by washing them through the soil.

Leader The main dominant shoot or stem of a plant (usually the terminal shoot).

Leaf mold A compost-like substance formed from partially decomposed leaves.

Legume A member of the pea family.

Lime An alkaline substance formed from calcium.

Loam A soil that has equal proportions of clay, sand, and silt.

Mulch A layer of material applied to cover the soil in order to block out light and help trap moisture.

Multirow system A method of growing plants close together to regulate their overall size and to control weeds.

Nutrients The minerals (fertilizers) used to feed plants.

Nitrogenous A fertilizer or manure containing nitrogen, which is important for plant growth.

Organic Materials that are derived from decomposed animal or plant remains.

Outdoor storage A method of storing produce outside, but with some protection.

Overwinter Keeping a plant alive through the winter, usually by protecting it from frost.

Peat Decayed sphagnum mosses, or rushes and sedges.

Perennial Any plant that has a life cycle of more than three years.

Pesticide A chemical used to control pests. It is also a broad, generic name for chemicals used in the garden to control pests, diseases, and weeds.

pH A measure of acidity and alkalinity in a soil.

Potting Transferring a plant to a larger container, or transferring young plants or seedlings from the seedbed/tray to a larger container.

Propagation Techniques used to multiply a number of plants.

Propagator A structure used to propagate plants, or a person who propagates plants.

Pruning The practice of cutting plants to improve their growth or train them to grow in a certain way.

Raised bed system Growing plants in beds of soil above soil level so that they root deeper in the soil.

Rambler A vigorous trailing plant with a rambling growth pattern.

Restoration pruning A pruning system that is based on the systematic replacement of lateral fruiting branches.

Rhizome A specialized underground stem that lies horizontally in the soil.

Root The underground support system of a plant.

Rootball The combined root system and surrounding soil/compost of a plant.

Rootstock The root system onto which a cultivar is budded or grafted.

Runner A stem that grows horizontally close to the ground.

Sap The juice, or "blood," of a plant.

Scale A modified leaf of a bulb used for propagation purposes.

Scion The propagation material that is taken from a cultivar or variety in order to be used for budding or grafting.

Shrub A woody, stemmed plant.

Side shoot A stem arising from a branch stem or twig.

Spindlebush A fruit tree grown into a broadly pyramidal shape to allow all of the fruit to receive maximum sunlight.

Spur A short fruit or flower-bearing branch.

Stone fruits A term usually reserved for fruit-bearing members of the genus *Prunus* (e.g., apricot, cherry, damson, and plum).

Stopping Cutting out the growing point of a shoot to encourage the development of lateral shoots.

Storage A method of keeping plants in an environment that delays ripening and decay.

Subsoil The layers of soil beneath the topsoil.

Sucker A shoot arising from below ground level.

Taproot The large main root of a plant.

Tender A plant that is killed or damaged by low temperatures (50° F).

Tendril A thin, twining stemlike structure used by some climbing plants to support themselves.

Terminal bud The uppermost bud in the growing point of a stem (also known as the "apical bud").

Thinning The removal of branches to improve the quality of those that remain.

Tilth A fine, crumbly layer of surface soil.

Top dressing An application of fertilizer or bulky organic matter that is added to the soil surface and often incorporated around the base of the plant.

Training The practice of making plants grow into a particular shape or pattern.

Transplanting Moving plants from one growing area to another in order to provide them with more growing room.

Truss A compact cluster of flowers or fruit growing on one stalk.

Tuber A root or stem modified to form a storage organ.

Tying down A method of using string ties for training shoots into a horizontal position.

Variegated Plant parts (usually leaves) marked with a blotched pattern of colors on top of a base color of green.

Vegetative growth Nonflowering stem growth.

Virus A harmful, debilitating organism that lives inside the plant and for which there is no cure.

Waterlogging A condition in soil where all of the air spaces are filled (saturated) with water, and oxygen is excluded as a result.

Wilt The partial collapse of a plant due to water loss or root damage.

Wind rock The loosening of a plant's roots caused by wind.

Wound Any cut or damaged area on a plant.

index

Page numbers in italics refer to illustrations.

Planting zones map

This map shows how the countries can be divided up by minimum winter temperatures. The zones are based on the United States Department of Agriculture planting zones.

KEY TO PLANT ZONES

The numbers/symbols used in the plant portraits in chapter 10 indicate the approximate optimum temperature range that each plant prefers to grow well. Used in conjunction with this map, these zones will enable you to plan which crops will produce average or above average yields in your garden.

ZONE 1
BELOW -50° F

ZONE 2
-50° F to -40° F

ZONE 3
-40° F to -30° F

ZONE 4
-30° F TO -20° F

ZONE 5
-20° F to -10° F

ZONE 6
-10° F to 0° F

ZONE 7
0° F to 10° F

ZONE 8
10° F to 20° F

ZONE 9
20° F to 30° F

ZONE 10
30° F to 40° F

Zone 11
ABOVE 40° F

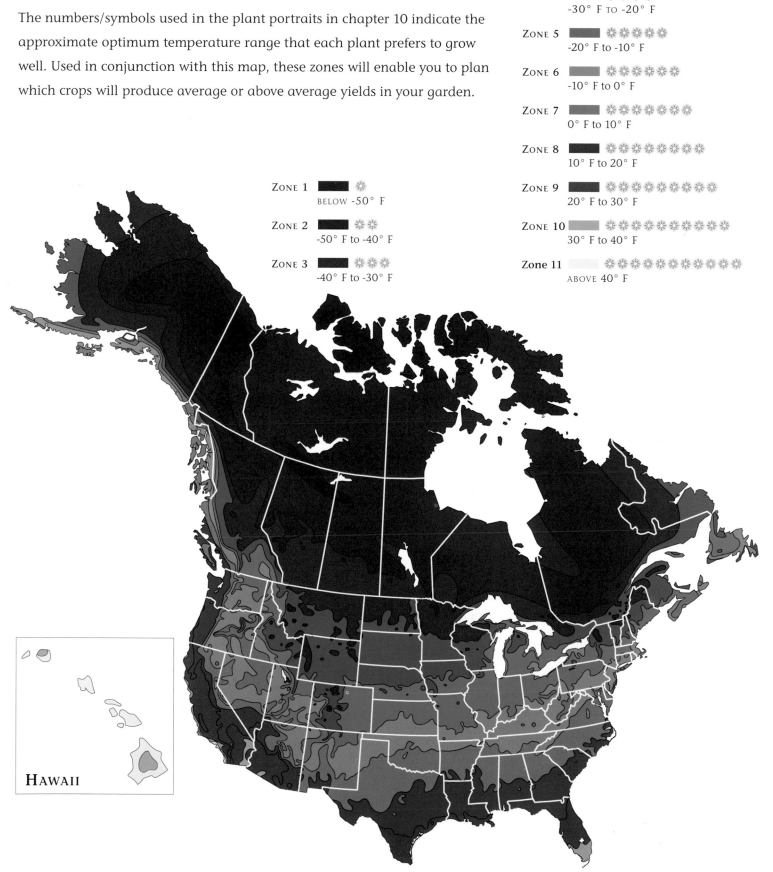

HAWAII

acknowledgments

Steven Bradley "I would like to thank my wife Val Bradley for her help with the text, Iain MacGregor for his help and encouragement, Mark Winwood for his photographic skills and sense of humor, and David Kenyon, Julie Ryan, and all of the gardening and technical staff at Capel Manor College and *Gardening Which*."

Jo Whitworth would like to thank those concerned for allowing her to take photographs in the following locations: Barleywood, Hants; Darkley House, Norton Canon, Herefordshire; Harroway Organic Farm, Whitchurch, Hants; HDRA Organic Gardens, Ryton; Holt Farm, Blagdon, Somerset; Hookeswood House, Farnham, Dorset; Lady Farm, Chelwood, Somerset; Longmead House, Longparish, Hants; Little Court, Crawley, Hants; Longstock Park Nursery, Stockbridge, Hants; March End, Sherfield English, Hants; Melplash Court, Melplash, Dorset; RHS Flower Show, Chelsea: Gardens Sans Frontieres/Designer Ryl Nowell; RHS Flower Show, Hampton Court: Go Organic Garden/Designer Land Art; RHS Gardens, Wisley and Rosemoor; Rose Cottage, Bordon, Hants; Somerset Lodge, Petworth, W. Sussex; Secretts PYO and Farm Shop, Milford, Surrey; Steve Jordan and Sarah Morgan, St. Mary Bourne, Hants; Titsey Place Gardens, Surrey; West Dean Gardens, Chichester, Sussex; Ulvik, Winchester, Hants; Watercroft, Penn, Buckinghamshire; West Green House, Hartlepool.

The U.K. publisher would like to thank the following:
Capel Manor College, Enfield, Middlesex; West Dean Gardens, Wyevale Garden Centres Plc, King's Acre Road, Hereford, for the loan of tools and equipment; *Gardening Which* Magazine.

Laurel Glen Publishing
An imprint of the Advantage Publishers Group
5880 Oberlin Drive, San Diego, CA 92121-4794
www.advantagebooksonline.com

Copyright © Text, illustrations, and design, Murdoch Books (U.K.) Ltd., 2001

All photography © Jo Whitworth except the following: Colin Carver/Nature Photographers Ltd., p189br; E.A. Janes/Nature Photographers Ltd., p188tr; Howard Rice (with thanks to Mr. & Mrs. Reeve)/The Garden Picture Library p159; Paul Sterry/Nature Photographers Ltd., p189bl; Lauren Shear © Murdoch Books (U.K.) Ltd. p71.

All project photography by Mark Winwood © Murdoch Books (U.K.) Ltd.

All notations of errors or omissions should be addressed to Laurel Glen Publishing, editorial department, at the above address. All other correspondence (author inquiries, permissions, and rights) concerning the content of this book should be addressed to Murdoch Books (U.K.) Ltd., Ferry House, 51-57 Lacy Road, Putney, London SW15 1PR, U.K.

Library of Congress Cataloging-in-Publication Data

Bradley, Steven
  Garden harvest / Steven Bradley with photography by Jo Whitworth.
    p. cm.
  ISBN 1-57145-763-1
  1. Gardening. 2. Fruit-culture. 3. Vegetable gardening. I. Title

SB453 .B686 2002
635--dc21

Printed in Hong Kong by Toppan.
1 2 3 4 5 06 05 04 03 02

Every effort has been made to ensure that the photography, illustrations, and text are accurate at the time of going to press.